Soccer Transition Training

For Tony DiCicco and Anson Dorrance–

World Cup champions and American soccer coaching legends

Soccer Transition Training

Moving Between Attack and Defense

Tony Englund | John Pascarella

Meyer & Meyer Sport

British Library in Cataloguing Publication Data
A catalogue record for this book is available from the British Library

Soccer Transition Training
Maidenhead: Meyer & Meyer Sport (UK) Ltd., 2019
ISBN: 978-1-78255-151-5

Aachen, Auckland, Beirut, Cairo, Cape Town, Dubai, Hägendorf, Hong Kong, Indianapolis, Manila, New Delhi, Singapore, Sydney, Tehran, Vienna
Member of the World Sports Publishers' Association (WSPA), www.w-s-p-a.org
Printed by Print Consult GmbH, Munich, Germany

ISBN: 978-1-78255-151-5
Email: info@m-m-sports.com
www.m-m-sports.com

CONTENTS

FOREWORD

There are a lot of soccer coaching manuals out there. It is difficult to tell one from the other, to be honest. There are bad ones, and good ones, and really good ones. I've been coaching in youth and professional soccer for the last 25 years. When I look for a book on soccer, I progress through a list of what I find important. I start with the coaching ability of the author. Not all great coaches make great authors, and not all great authors make great coaches. But I've found that exercises and drills from a coach who has been on the field trying to develop his players under some type of pressure tend to resonate better with me. That has been my experience. Whether I'm coaching a professional team where my job hangs on the weekend's result or I'm working with an energetic u12 boys team that I know is on the verge of exploding, I coach under pressure. External and internal pressure is what motivates all good coaches, and when I pick up a coaching book, I want the author to have experienced that pressure. Next, I look for a book that is easy to read and well organized. I want to be able to jump from exercise to exercise without confusion. I want drills that stand alone, and I want a progression of ideas that build on each other. If a coaching book is going to be useful to me, it must be utilitarian and functional. Lastly, I look at the quality of the soccer exercises in the book. Do they make sense? Are they easily replicated? Is there room for me to tweak them and make them more useful to my particular team? In Tony Englund and John Pascarella's new book, *Soccer Transition Training: Moving Between Attack and Defense*, all three characteristics of a good soccer manual are satisfied in spades.

I have coached with and against Tony and John. I've seen their teams play incredibly well with all their players knowing their roles and responsibilities innately. I've also seen their teams clunk and grind to a halt due to lethargy or the opponent or whatever makes teams lie down from time to time. And on every occasion, they treat their players and their opponents with respect. They seek to educate, progress the entire group, and help their players enjoy the moments good and bad. The internal and external pressure is seen only in their eagerness to put their team back on the field to improve on the great performances or the poor ones. These are my type of coaches.

Soccer Transition Training is a colorful and easily accessible book. From the table of contents to the bibliography, the exercises are organized in a sensible way. The book flows with exercises that build on each other or stand alone as needed. Browse through it, and you'll see for yourself.

The most important part of a coaching book is the content. The content of *Soccer Transition Training* is thorough, creative, insightful, and exciting. Coaching transition in soccer is not easy to do. I've seen professional coaches who have struggled putting together a cogent training session on transition. We coach offense well. We coach defense well. We coach set-pieces well. But coaching how we go from defense to offense, or defense to offense... we tend to leave these to competitive games or scrimmages. We expect that the game will naturally teach our players to transition through these phases of the game. But soccer has evolved. The speed and athleticism of the modern game demands that we teach our players how to be defensively organized while we are in possession. We have to be willing to defend in a low bloc but be ready to get into the attacking third in a few passes. This book will help you do that. The exercises are enjoyable. They are easy to replicate. They are simple *and* advanced. Enjoy the book, the exercises, and the explanations. Soccer is an ageless wonder that we can all enjoy for many more years to come, and this book adds to the pantheon of strong and effective soccer books that will help us do so.

–Amos Magee
Director, Player Personnel
Minnesota United FC (MLS)

ACKNOWLEDGMENTS

This project has been a labor of learning. My previous writing endeavors have largely been an effort to catalogue what I have seen and learned over a quarter century of intensive soccer coaching. As such, I always felt that I was writing from a position of strength, with plenty of material and a firm grasp of the central issues, from goalkeeping to systems of play.

The decision to try to characterize and explore the teaching of the nature of transition in the modern game was, for me, tantamount to trying find one's way out of the deep woods without a useful map. At first consideration, there is a lot of nebulous discussion on the subject, but no coherent, thorough treatment of transition in coaching journals, books or licensing courses. Yet this was a subject that begged to be explored. Watch any high-level match, and the analysis will most often include one team's ability (or inability) to transition as a decisive factor. Indeed, the coaching community is now rife with stars who espouse counterpressing and counterattacking.

Knowing that this would be an effort to go into unchartered territory, I have relied more heavily on discussions with colleagues than in my past efforts, and I am thankful for the patience and input of all who had a hand in influencing this study.

I want to begin by thanking the staff at Meyer & Meyer. Writing and publishing can be a bit of an adventure under any circumstances, but from Editor-in-Chief Manuel Morschel to our editorial contacts Liz Evans and Kristina Oltrogge, the staff have been without fail helpful and supportive, and John and I are very thankful for the opportunity to publish our work with Meyer & Meyer.

Nathan Klonecki, the director of coaching at St. Croix Soccer Club, has long been first and foremost a good friend, and also my favorite conversationalist for philosophical discussions about soccer. We see the game differently, but we share a passion for learning and for teaching, and his insights color my understanding of all the topics discussed herein.

Mike Huber, with whom I have coached championship teams for the past 3 years, is the perfect pairing for me in a coaching sense. His sharp sense of humor and lighthearted approach to coaching make the job much more fun, and he has a knack for finding the right exercise at the right time. He, too, has contributed much to the ideas presented here.

Casey Holm, the remarkably driven and successful high-school, club, and college coach, went out of his way to contribute several specific exercises, and I am thankful for his ideas and our collaboration on the field.

Mike Kelleher, Kor Cha, Simon Whitehead, Thom Peer, Tim Magnuson, Matt Carlson, Mark Yueill, Wayne Harrison, and Phil Walczak are all colleagues who have added to my coaching philosophy and also my enjoyment of coaching over the years.

Jeff Tipping and Ian Barker, successive directors of coaching education for the NSCAA (now United Soccer Coaches), have both gone out of their way on numerous occasions to support both my soccer-coaching education and my writing projects, and I am very thankful for their efforts both on my behalf and for the American soccer-coaching community.

Amos Magee of Minnesota United FC took time-out of his hectic MLS preseason schedule to contribute the Foreword to this book. I have observed Amos as a player for many years with the Minnesota Thunder and through his work as a coach at the youth and MLS level. He absolutely radiates authenticity and soccer intelligence, and I am thankful for his participation here.

I met Tony DiCicco on several occasions and was always impressed with his sincerity and his commitment to soccer coaching, particularly to the causes of goalkeeper coaching and the advancement of women's soccer coaching. He is missed and remembered in the coaching community.

Anson Dorrance to whom, along with Tony DiCicco, this book is dedicated, is a giant among soccer coaches. I have had the opportunity to meet and work with Anson on a handful of occasions, and I always walk away moved by his approachability, his distinctive, driven, and confident voice, his belief in the importance of a competitive mentality and his unshakeable commitment to his program and to American soccer coaching.

John Pascarella continues to be an inspiration for me both on and off the field. His energy, optimism, intellectual curiosity, and sense of humor are all very contagious, and the time we spent writing this book together has for me served to reinforce the feeling that coaching can be the most enjoyable of pursuits.

Tess Wilder and Jake Wilder are my stepchildren. They have now spent the better part of a decade with me as their "not dad," and their patience with me as I tried to find my role in their lives is something I appreciate more each day. I am proud of both of you.

I would be remiss if I failed to thank my parents Tony and Carole Englund for their unfailing support of me and my coaching projects. Through all my playing and coaching experience and education, my dad has been the most outstanding coach–on and off the field–I have encountered. As this book goes to print, my dad is facing a series of complicated heart surgeries, and I have spent much time in recent weeks thinking about how much both he and my mom sacrificed so that my brother, my sister, and I could enjoy elite sports and a happy, supportive family environment as children, and how much both Dad and Mom mean to me. Throughout my journey, they have been shining examples of how to live one's life.

My wife Beth has been a constant source of encouragement and support as I waded into and through this subject. I often marvel at her patience with all my soccer pursuits, and I am forever thankful that she chooses to share in and support these endeavors.

–Tony Englund

Soccer Transition Training could not have been possible without the help of many people along the way: my wife Lisa and four children, Kara, Cassie, John-Patrick, and Jordan, who somehow always manage to deal with Dad's schedule and time constraints, already tight based on coaching and made tighter by writing. My parents, Gabriel and Antoinette Pascarella, who have always been tremendously supportive of my life in the game from an early age through old age (I'm actually only fifty-one, but it seems old on certain days). Our publisher, Meyer & Meyer, who must have liked our first book enough to let us write a second. My coaching colleagues—Amos Magee, Ashley Wallace, Davey Arnaud, Ian Barker, and Percy Hoff—each of whom contributed to our refining and now promotion of the book. Finally, I'd like to thank Tony Englund for the opportunity to collaborate with him on this book and on our first, *Soccer Goalkeeper Training—The Comprehensive Guide.* If it wasn't for his persistence and guidance, I probably would not have understood the difficulties of writing and the joy that comes with finishing a project like this!! I hope you all enjoy reading this book as much as I have enjoyed the process of contributing to it.

–John Pascarella

Introduction

TRANSITION AT THE HEART OF SOCCER COACHING IN THE MODERN GAME

In the summer of 2015, I was granted the opportunity, through the National Soccer Coaches Association of America's Master Coach Certificate program, to spend several days watching first-team training and matches at Sporting Kansas City in Major League Soccer (MLS). The experience was outstanding, and I remain thankful to the entire first-team staff, and particularly John Pascarella, for the opportunity to talk to them at length about all manner of coaching intricacies and observe their work.

Interestingly, one of the seminal moments of that summer visit was the opportunity to attend an MLS match between Sporting and the Vancouver Whitecaps. At the time, Vancouver was sitting atop the Western Conference standings and Sporting was in the midst of a bit of a late season swoon, saddled with significant injuries and a lot of fatigued players. The game itself was a crazy back-and-forth battle, with Sporting winning on an injury-time goal.

However, what really struck me was the varying tactics of the two teams. Despite the undeniable success of the league, MLS teams' tactics are often fairly bland, with most teams still not featuring the often-brilliant attacking personalities who highlight the tactics of major European clubs and leagues. Most MLS teams are well organized and defend with a lot of players behind the ball, playing very low-risk soccer. That said, Sporting Kansas City, under its outstanding manager Peter Vermes, plays a 4-3-3 and tries to press the ball all over the field. It creates a lot of turnovers and typically spends much of the game in its opponent's half of the field. If there is a weakness to Sporting's tactics over the past several years, it's that it is often vulnerable to counterattacks because its shape pushes a lot of men forward and spreads them across the field. Its pressing also wears down its players over the course of the season, and the match, too, creating opportunities for counterattacking opponents.

Vancouver, by contrast, is set up in a 4-4-2 at the time, and it was extremely apparent that its back six (four-man back line and two holding midfielders) were simply assigned to hold their shape and win the ball back for the four attacking personalities. It was also striking to see the speed and directness of Vancouver's play when it won possession.

The match left an indelible impression upon me regarding the importance of transitional moments in soccer. Sporting clearly thinks in terms of wanting the ball at its players' feet, grinding down an opponent, and winning the ball as high up the field as often as possible. Vancouver, however, was geared to absorb pressure while not conceding a lot of opportunities and then strike at a moment's notice, catching the opponent out.

Certainly, these contrasting tactics have been popular across the world for many years and in higher-profile matches in Europe and at the World Cup, but the game was a sharp microcosm of the two predominant tactical philosophies in the world today, namely that of teams that want to use the ball to wear down and exploit an opponent (e.g., Guardiola's FC Barcelona) or teams (e.g., Jose Mourinho's Chelsea) that "park the bus," get lots of players behind the ball and then burst forward with a few key players to score a counterattacking goal. To be sure, there are many variations of both schools, and some of the best teams in the world find a wonderful balance (e.g., champions Germany at the 2016 World Cup).

However, whether it's the evolution of tactics in MLS or the Premier League, it is clear that whereas the paramount tactical discussion in high-level soccer 20 years ago was about systems of play and, relatedly, *style*, there is clearly today a greater emphasis on trying to prepare players to exploit situations and, particularly, *transitional moments* in soccer.

This book evolved from the realization that despite the transitional emphasis in soccer coaching, there is very little in print to help coaches share ideas about how to manage these moments. In preparation for writing this book, we reviewed all the relevant literature available, including major biographies of leading coaches such as Pep Guardiola, Alex Ferguson, Jose Mourinho, Johan Cruyff, Arsene Wenger, Marcelo Bielsa, and others (please see the Bibliography for specific references). We also consulted more than a dozen professional, college, and club coaches on the subject. We watched hundreds of hours of video, reviewing tactics on both sides of the ball in World Cup qualifying, La Liga, the Premier League, the Bundesliga, and MLS. Finally, as high-level club, high-school, college, and professional coaches of more than 25 years, we also reviewed all the sessions, match plans, scouting, and coaching school information we have compiled.

The result is a thorough, and, hopefully, groundbreaking study of the nature and teaching of transition in the modern game. High-level coaches will find many examples of all kinds of transition exercises and games, from 1 vs. 1 grid duels to 11 vs. 11 conditioned games, all designed to flesh out and improve your team's understanding of and effectiveness in dominating transition. For newer coaches, the work also helps lay out the nature of transition in both directions, providing teaching cues and a broad understanding of the critical concepts needed to execute the team's chosen transition philosophy.

This book also pushes the proverbial envelope regarding the idea of transition to encompass two relatively revolutionary ideas.

1. Transition after the whistle. How many games hinge on the outcome of set-pieces? The team that can master the *mental transition* required to execute an attacking set-piece or fight off a defending set-piece is often the winner. The book therefore offers a chapter on these critical transition moments, emphasizing mental preparation, conditioned exercises, and more.

2. Transition *through time* in the game. This idea highlights the need to prepare our players to deal with situational challenges throughout a match. Statistically, a remarkable

number (some estimate as many as 75 percent) of goals are scored in the opening or last 5 minutes of a half, or after a goal is scored. This situation, as well as unexpected transitional moments including injuries, disciplinary cards, bad calls, weather, and more conventional challenges such as playing with a lead or a deficit through time phases in the game are all transitional in the sense that the dynamics of the match change with the occurrence of and/or the movement through time phases in the match. Therefore, this book will offer a discussion of these critical moments with the idea that the coach must prepare the team to cope with and exploit these situations.

Some notes regarding the material:

- Sizes of playing areas are often omitted. This is a purposeful decision, because it is important that the coach adjust the grids and playing areas to fit the needs of the players and the exercise. In all cases, the coach must be constantly attuned to the need to tweak the playing environment to maximize learning and challenge the players.
- There is an emphasis in the material on efficiency in training. Economical training is ideal in any case, and this is particularly true where repetitions will be few because of time constraints, training load, and difficulty in recreating match conditions (and large-scale pressing and counterattacking moves definitively qualify in this sense). Thus, it is important for the coach to attend to details (i.e., ball supply and the number of players involved) to make training as efficient as possible for the players.
- This volume is both a theoretical examination of transitional moments and also an *idea* book featuring dozens of examples of useful training exercises on all aspects of the subject. It is important to note that though the exercises are usually presented in a progressive manner, with few exceptions they are not laid out in complete sessions. Rather, the coach can pick and choose and find the right exercises for his team based on design, need, opponent, and training numbers.

The hope is that this book provides a wide-ranging, easily accessible means from which coaches of every level can refine their own philosophy regarding transition and an idea book from which coaches can pick and choose to make training on transition both interesting and effective.

Chapter 1

THE FOUR MOMENTS... PLUS TWO?

Jeff Tipping, the director of coaching education emeritus for the National Soccer Coaches Association of America (now United Soccer Coaches), opened a brilliant session at the National Convention many years ago by quoting French coaching legend Gerard Houllier.

Houllier, Tipping explained, defined soccer tactics based on four moments.

1. Our team has the ball.
2. Our team has just lost the ball.
3. The opponent has the ball.
4. Our team has just won the ball.

It is useful to view these tactics in a continuous, circular fashion.

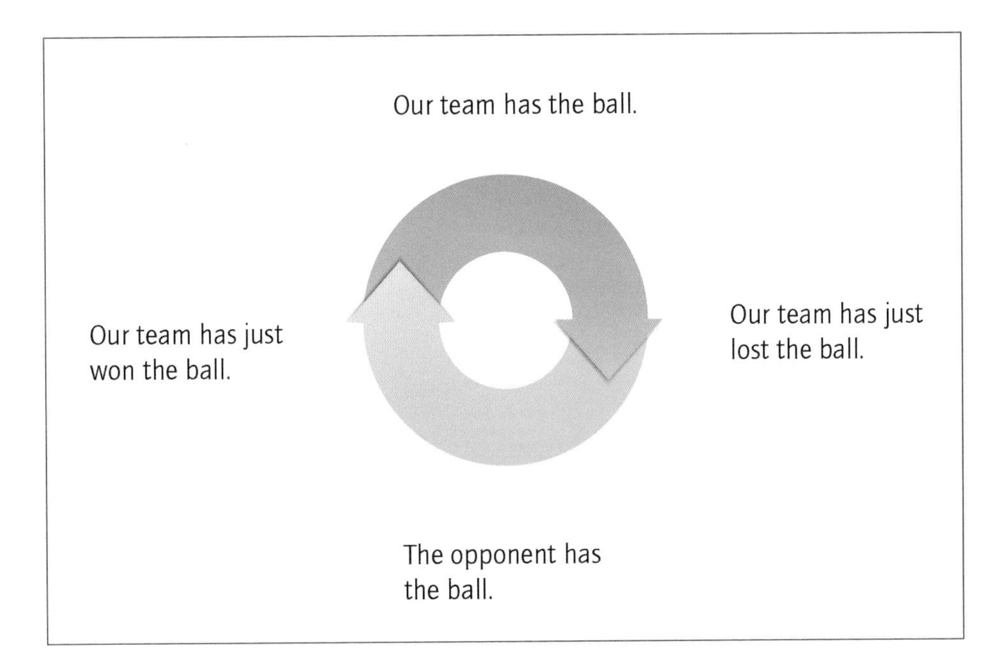

Tipping went on to present a session on counterattacking that targeted the fourth moment, that is, what to do when the ball is won. Given the evolution of soccer tactics outlined in the Introduction, this was an especially prescient presentation. The game, particularly at the professional club and international levels, is now analyzed based on the principles outlined by Houllier and emphasized by Tipping.

As transitional moments gain more emphasis, one of the results has been a dramatic increase in the premium placed on tactical speed. The game is now played at a stunningly fast pace in transition in particular.

As a result, it's interesting to note that tactical thinking is arguably now creating an extra pair of critical moments. First, the notion that our team has just lost the ball can be augmented with "our team is about to lose the ball." This distinction is important in the sense that if coaches can imprint upon their teams the ability *read* the game to the point of anticipating the team's loss of possession, the implications for the team's transition will offer a great advantage. For example, if a center back sees that his long pass to the center striker will be intercepted and begins to recover immediately, he may aid his team in covering up before the opponent can seize the moment. Similarly, if players recognize the moment when possession is about to be won, a number of advantages accrue, from supporting runs and communication to penetrating attacking runs.

Think of the implications for teams and for the game if players consistently read play based on an understanding of the requirements for their position, line, and team for each shade of tactical shift throughout the match!

Thus, this book will propose that teams and players recognize *six* critical moments recurring throughout the match.

1. Our team has the ball.
2. Our team is about to lose the ball.
3. Our team has just lost the ball.
4. The opponent has the ball.
5. Our team is about to win the ball.
6. Our team has just won the ball.

It is important to note that some coaches will consider that the added moments—anticipating transition—either cloud the issue or will lead to players bailing out early on attacks or abandoning defensive assignments too early because they think that their team will win the ball. This is all well and good from the standpoint of philosophical discussion, and we spent much time debating as to whether it is desirable or even necessary to include the extra two moments.

Our conclusion: The philosophical discussion of the added moments is worthwhile in the sense that it highlights the ongoing trend toward speed and especially speed in transition in the game. Whatever one's opinion regarding the utility of the added moments, most will agree that the ability to read the game with more speed can only add to the pace at which our players and teams transition, augmenting their collective success.

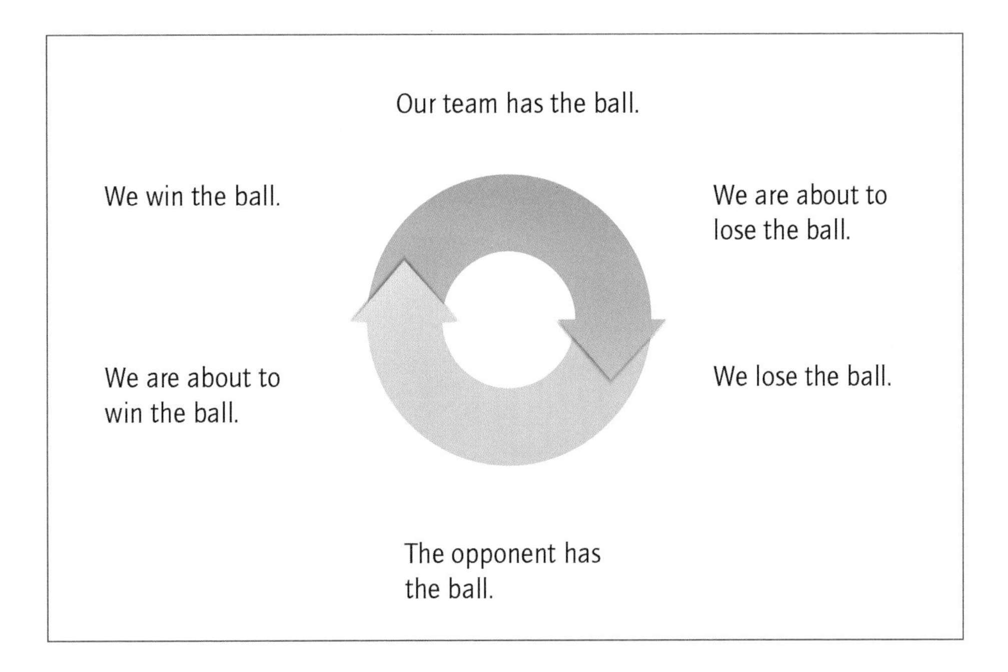

Given that so much energy is now invested in developing players, teams, and tactics that can exploit the opportunities presented by transitional moments (pressing and counterattacking in particular), it is time for a more detailed look at how these elements influence the game, and how we can best educate players and coaches to master these situations.

Chapter 2

THE TEAM IS ABOUT TO LOSE THE BALL

Soccer, perhaps more than any other major sport, features frequent changes in possession. The movement to and from possession for each team is known as *transition*. Negative transition is the act of losing the ball, whereas positive transition is the act of winning the ball.

Many coaches devote some training to counterattacking (from positive transition). Fewer trainers devote much time to negative transition. Fewer still are well versed in coaching their teams to *anticipate* negative transition and therefore be prepared to maximize potential advantages accrued from speedy, structured transition.

How can we help players understand and anticipate negative transition? The crucial point of emphasis here is the *anticipation* factor. It has been consistently pointed out to me in tactical discussions with colleagues that we do not want players bailing out on attacking patterns because they *think* possession will be lost. To wit, a winger should not bail out on his run to the back post just because he doesn't like the quality of the cross from his opposite-side winger. He needs to complete his run, on the off chance that the ball ricochets and finds its way to him.

However, if that cross is blocked, and it is clear that the ball will fall at the feet of an unpressured defender far from the runner, the winger *should* adjust his run to take into account the likely change of possession and the advantage of his taking away a long switch to the opposing back on his side of the field.

What would you hope your players would do in these similar situations? How would you *coach* your players to respond?

- A long ball is served forward from your back line. Though your center forward is in the area where the ball will land, he will clearly not win the race to the ball, and the defender from the other team will corral the ball, have time to look up, and probably distribute the ball forward. How far should your players continue to push out? How early would you have them resort to a defending shape?
- Your team takes a corner kick. The ball is flicked on past the far post toward the far corner flag, where an opposing player will be the first to arrive. Your players can arrive to press, but the possibility of a clearance and counter is at least even. Will your players know your preferences?
- You are playing a team that keys on counterattacking opportunities and is very good at the long ball to their speedy front-runners. Your team has been beaten several times this season by similar attacks. How does this affect your preparation for this opponent?

Clearly, there are shades of decision-making that players need to learn if they are going to make good choices to support their team in transition, and because the right choice may become the wrong choice in the matter of a few seconds, making good, early decisions will impact the performance and fortunes of the team.

The other aspect of negative transition that is very challenging for coaches working with young players in particular is the natural letdown associated with the loss of possession.

What is the mentality of the team when a mistake is made? A casual survey of professional fixtures, to say nothing of youth and college matches, produces a wide range of reactions to the likely loss of possession. In our own coaching, we have had players who are defined by their ball winning and who redouble their efforts when it appears possession will be lost. We have also seen top players at all levels who simply shut down for a few seconds when it appears the team will lose possession.

Without a doubt, one of the greatest mental challenges in soccer coaching is helping players identify and embrace the notion that the moment when possession is lost is an opportunity to win back the ball.

Thiago Silva of Paris St.-Germain battles for the ball in transition against Malmo FF in UEFA Champions League play.

A player's willingness to defend as soon as possession is lost is almost always directly correlated to their investment in the team.
–Unknown

Some examples from our own coaching journals:

- A through-pass is played too long and early and rolls to the opposing goalkeeper.

  Reaction: Many players turning their backs to the ball and lamenting the loss of possession.

  Solution: If all eleven players use the time when the ball is rolling to the opposing goalkeeper to begin to position to win it back, they will often already be in position to defend when the goalkeeper finally distributes.

- A player fails to see the next pass and dribbles into a pair of defenders, is upended, and the other team wins possession.

  Reaction: Teammates critique the oversight by the player in possession rather than preparing to win back the ball.

  Solution: Build the player back up by encouraging him to see the next pass when he's in that position again. Do this verbally while moving quickly to support defensive transition. Use the time when it appears possession will be lost to position oneself to win it back after the tackle.

- An attacker fails to corral a speculative pass forward, and his first touch appears to set up the opposition.

  Reaction: The attacking flow of the team shuts down as players are disappointed with the attacker's touch.

  Solution: Can the ball be won in spite of the poor touch? If not, avoid losing precious seconds lamenting the need to defend, and start to move to a defending posture as the ball is travelling.

Clearly, these moments occur hundreds of times in every match. Soccer is a game of mistakes where possession often shifts after just a few seconds. Think of the time lost to the team when it's clear that possession will be lost, but rather than spring forward to the next tactical opportunity, the team should pause and then slowly recoil to defend.

From a coaching perspective, the challenge is to be vigilant and disciplined in seeking opportunities to help players and the team to transition more quickly. Given that this is a mental skill, the emphasis in training is on *identifying* these moments in the flow of the session and reminding players to avoid relaxing in any way when it appears possession will be lost.

Here are some general suggestions as to how to create and coach these moments in the training environment:

- Virtually all the field exercises in chapter III (The Team Loses the Ball) begin with a turnover.
    1. Take the opportunity to talk with players at training about what they are thinking about at the moment when the ball will be turned over. Are they ready? Can they adjust their positioning in anticipation of the turnover? What is their communication in each situation as it appears possession will be lost? What is their mentality? Can you, as the coach, impact players' thinking to help them see the impending loss of possession as an opportunity, requiring continued, sustained effort from the entire group?
    2. Be creative. Add another pass to the opening sequence in possession to build the sense of anticipation that the ball will be lost, or play with one team only trying to hold possession, with the inevitable result that it will turn over the ball. How do the players react? Are they moving to defend even as the turnover approaches?
- Freeze play in a playing environment. From there, the coach can either set up and/or coach through the mental requirements for rapid transition. Be careful to avoid making the stop a habit, as it is counterintuitive to trying to get players to analyze on the go and play at speed.
- Hold a brief discussion with players about the advantages of recognizing approaching transition.
    1. Ask them to identify *how* the ball is turned over (make sure to list many examples).

2. Ask them how they feel when possession is lost or about to be lost. Most will admit to letting down a bit. Coach them to understand that this is normal, but not necessary. Instead, the team must be motivated to win back the ball.

3. What is their first thought when possession is about to be lost? Some will tune out or be upset with the player who is turning over the ball. Identify these reactions as normal, but unacceptable. Everyone loses possession. Time spent being disappointed is time lost in a match. It is important to recognize that losing possession happens at every position and that winning back the ball is the responsibility of the entire team.

- Record a training game or match and review the footage with the team, looking specifically at the team's reaction when possession is lost. This can be a tough pill for some players to swallow, and it's important to avoid singling out players and pointing out their errors. Rather, this is an exercise in observing player reactions to the imminent loss of possession. Done right, this is a nearly foolproof (the tape does not lie) means of identifying players' reactions when possession is about to be lost.

    1. Common reactions
        a. Failure to recover.
        b. Effort stops.
        c. Negative body language (head down, kick the grass, hand gestures, shoulders drop).
        d. Negative communication.
        e. A few seconds of sustained effort to win back the ball and then the player shuts down.
        f. A response that is not coordinated with teammates to win back the ball as soon as possible.

Take the opportunity to talk about how each of these reactions affects the team's ability to transition, highlighting the difference to be expected if everyone reacted immediately and positively to the new challenge when the ball is lost.

For advanced coaches and teams, it is necessary to carry the discussion through some of the positive results to be gained through momentary negative transition. Regardless of the opponent, every team goes through some level of adjustment when the ball is lost or won. Therefore, when the opponents win the ball, they will usually be vulnerable for a brief moment before settling into possession or striking at your team. In that moment, your team has the opportunity to win back the ball and perhaps catch the opponent shifting to or from a more open, attacking stance. Elite players and teams understand this distinction and embrace the opportunity to win the transition battle by being the team to shift more quickly and smoothly to and from attacking and defending.

Positive team transition: sample view of team expanding shape in possession

Negative team transition: sample view of team compacting shape in transition

5 vs. 5 plus 1: Reading the Imminent Loss of Possession

This is a base teaching exercise for helping players to think about reading an imminent loss of possession. Play 5 vs. 5 plus 1 neutral *defender* and goalkeepers on one half of the field, narrowed to the width of the 18-yard box. If the neutral defender wins the ball, he passes to the team that had been defending, then changes teams. Restarts come from the goalkeepers to keep the game flowing.

COACHING POINTS

- The extra defender is incorporated to give the defenders a numerical advantage and create situations where it becomes clear before the event that possession will be lost to the attacking team. This will be a choppy game by definition, and one that should as such be played for a few minutes and then revisited in another session.

- As was outlined in the opening chapter, the transitional moment that needs to be elucidated here, recognizing the imminent loss of possession, is a *mental* target. Therefore, the coach has to get feedback on what the players are seeing as the game flows.

- There are fundamentally three stages to check in this game. The first stage is to get players to recognize the potential loss of possession. We want *individual* feedback, so at this stage a verbal cue is not useful, because the players will echo one another. Rather, simply require the players on the defending team to raise a hand briefly when they feel their team will probably lose the ball. The coach will need to stop the action on a few occasions early in the game to get feedback from some players (some who put their hand up, and some who did not) and to discuss some of the moments when it became clear they were going to transition to defense. Do those moments recur in the game (yes, they do)? How did they react individually (was this the right move)? Did their reaction help their team? Can they read the imminent loss of possession *earlier*?
- The second stage is *group recognition*. Once the players are recognizing and noting the signs of impending loss of possession, then it will be useful to start to build group recognition. Create a verbal cue, such as calling out one of the prominent colors in your team's kit (e.g., "Black!") when the players think the team will lose the ball. The idea now is that if one player recognizes the cue and the others follow suit, they can react together, proactively, and quickly.
- The third and final stage is to implement *group action*. Once the group verbal cue is being called, the coach can start to look at how the group should react. There is a lot of gray area here. We don't want players abandoning great runs forward because there *might* be a loss of possession. However, if it is clear that possession will be lost, particularly in the middle and back thirds, we do as coaches want our players to recognize trouble and then take precautionary steps to cover the team in case the ball is lost (see the example in the diagram on the previous page, where the red back has dribbled into a double-team near the touchline. His teammates begin to move to get under the ball in case, as appears likely, he is dispossessed).

- In general, the team should try to identify likely loss of possession and start to move to a defensive posture earlier than its opponents can shift to attacking. Sometimes that posture will mean getting goal-side and marking; at other times it may mean instantly pressuring the player who won the ball. Those priorities need to be clarified to the players on the training field.

Kevin De Bruyne of Manchester City appears unlikely to win this duel against a pair of Watford defenders in 2016.

Three-Team Transition Exercise

Three teams of four play for possession inside a grid divided in half by a cone line. Two teams are active, and each defends in one half of the grid. The third team plays as neutral bumpers on the ends of the grid as shown above. Thus, when a team is in possession in its attacking half, it enjoys a 6 vs. 4 advantage, and when the defending team wins the ball, it must try to play to a target on the far end of the grid in transition. The example above shows how this can be an exercise designed to help players anticipate the loss of possession and to teach them to avoid the pitfalls of slowing down when their team loses possession. In the diagram, a member of the yellow team has taken a poor touch, resulting in a loss of possession to the white team. The ball-winner for white is now looking to play an outlet pass to the far end of the grid. Note that the two yellow players nearest the center of the grid have already begun defensive runs and that their first instinct is to cut out the passing lanes to the far targets while they recover in that direction. Note also that the two yellow players nearest the ball move to pressure the player in possession, hoping to win the ball before it can be played to space. Restarts come from the coach at the side of the grid.

COACHING POINTS

- Defensive recognition. When negative transition is anticipated (i.e., when the attackers have a poor touch and the ball will be recovered by the other team), what is the posture and reaction of the team in transition? If there is a chance to win back the ball before the outlet pass can be played, the players should definitively try to win the ball immediately. If, however, the ball will clearly be lost and there is the possibility of an outlet pass, how quickly can the players on that team recover to defending positions?

- Coordination. What communication is desired as the team begins defensive transition? Clearly, identifying first, second, and third defender roles while the team covers the ground into the defending zones will increase the coordination and effectiveness of the defending.

6 vs. 4 To Anticipate a Turnover

In 6 vs. 4, with the team of six working to goal, the emphasis is on the defenders to rally to defending positions as early as possible, anticipating a turnover. The defending group tries to move forward in possession beyond the red cone line near midfield for a point. Compel the defenders to try to build out as usual and then recognize when possession will be lost. All restarts are from the goalkeeper. When the team of six wins the ball, they attack the goal.

COACHING POINTS

- Focus on the difference between attacking shape (previous), which is wider and designed to weaken defending pressure, and defending shape (following), which is intended to concentrate the group and make it difficult for opponents to have a direct path to goal. Note the narrowing of the team shape, as the outside backs pinch to protect the space in front of goal. Anticipating this movement when the ball will clearly be lost will speed the team's transition to defending.

PROGRESSION

- Add a countergoal(s) near the midfield stripe at which the team of four can finish. Providing a goal to play to will further incentivize this group and also focus the team of six, who do not want to concede goals.
- Add players to create more realistic simulations and training.
- Limit the number of passes or time in possession for the team of six to keep the focus on the group of four and its transition (more repetition).

6 vs. 4 Defensive transition (2): This figure shows the recovery runs of the group of four when possession is lost or about to be lost.

Chapter 3

THE TEAM LOSES THE BALL

Perhaps the most stunning changes in the modern game involve the evolution of defending. For a long time in soccer, defending was thought of in the most basic terms, with coaches emphasizing the physical aspects of defending over the technical and finer tactical points, as well as group and team organization.

During the early 1990s (i.e., the 1990 World Cup, which witnessed just 115 goals compared to 171 in 2014), there was much concern that the game was headed in a cynical direction, as teams developed complex and conservative team-defending schemes. Indeed, the Italian *catenaccio* (roughly translated as a chain or door bolt—a formidable and organized defense) was all the rage, and coaches bought books and tapes on zonal defending and tossed around terms like *restraining lines*. Hard-hitting back-line players worked with goalkeepers free to pick up back passes with their hands to stifle attacking initiative. It seemed for a short time that the power of attacking was being sucked from the game, and teams experimented with new formations and innovative attacking schemes to overcome teams defending in the *bloc*.

We have to have the ball. We're terrible without the ball. –Pep Guardiola (FC Barcelona)

The changing of the back-pass rule (1992) encouraged players and coaches to think about the merits of playing more aggressively and to pressure teams further up the pitch in the hope of winning the ball back earlier. This change also gradually created a new class of goalkeepers (Manuel Neuer comes to mind) who are much more comfortable playing behind the back line, trusted to play with their feet in support of the field players. The advent of goalkeepers with field-player technical qualities allowed coaches to also alter their defensive schemes to play higher up the field, leaving the space behind the back line, to varying extents, to the goalkeeper to clean up.

Beginning with France in 1998 and Germany 4 years later, the game has witnessed a return to more attacking tactics, from the resurgence in popularity of three-man forward systems to the emphasis on counterattacking. However, defending tactics have also remained at the forefront, and terms such as *pressing*, and *high-* and *low-pressure defending*, have become topics of discussion and training for many coaches.

Indeed, much more emphasis is now placed on defending at every level, and coaches such as Jurgen Klopp (Dortmund and now Liverpool) have built very successful teams around complex defensive schemes. More and more time is now devoted to defending topics at coaching schools and clinics as coaches learn to refine and impart their defensive philosophies to their teams. Central to all the ongoing evolution is the need to defend well when the team is at its most vulnerable, which is to say the moment when the ball is lost.

It is very clear that the first few seconds and first few passes after possession is lost are critical to defensive safety and relatedly to winning back the ball. Professional coaches now produce elaborate training sessions to share their defensive schemes with their players, all with an eye toward creating more cohesion in the defensive mentality and performance of their teams, and the emphasis is typically on a few cues designed to emphasize winning the ball back quickly wherever it is lost. This chapter looks at key defensive concepts and considerations to help coaches refine and share their defensive philosophy and then develops transitional defending from 1 vs. 1 grids to 11 vs. 11 conditioned games.

ORGANIZING A PRESSING DEFENSE: KEY CONCEPTS AND DISCUSSION POINTS

Improving defending immediately
improves a team by an order of magnitude.
–Jurgen Klopp

Indeed, Jurgen Klopp's Borussia Dortmund and now Liverpool teams have demonstrated that highly organized and aggressive team defending can dramatically improve results and confidence.

In planning a defensive strategy for one's team, the coach must flesh out his philosophy on a number of wide-ranging variables. How many players on each line? High or low pressure? Zonal defending or a mix of man and zone? High or low lines? These questions are answered based on the abilities of the team's players (i.e., if the team lacks speed and fitness, high-pressure defending may be difficult), the opponent(s), and the predispositions of the coach as to what type of defending he prefers. It's worth noting that the overall defending must be well matched with the team's attacking strategy as well. For example, a team that is built around deliberate buildup in possession, featuring technically proficient but not particularly fast players and deploying a single striker may opt not to play high-pressure defense, knowing that the team's characteristics and setup favor a more conservative defending approach. Here, then, are some key defending concepts that will shape team defending. When these concepts have been addressed, the team can then think in terms of how to defend *in transition* as well.

- *How many defenders on each line?* Today, most teams place four defenders on the back line, though isolated cases of three or five defenders are seen. Typically, those declaring they play with three have another player drop out of the midfield to supplement the back line when possession is lost or a threat materializes. Similarly, most teams place three, four, or five players in the midfield, and in this era of blurred lines, many systems blend responsibilities for positions depending on their players and the opponents. For example, holding midfielders often drop onto the back line to fill in when a center back is pulled wide. Withdrawn forwards often behave like attacking midfielders when the team defends. Whatever the arrangements by line, it's critical to understand the implications of these assignments for team tactics. For example, in a 4-2-3-1, which is very common today, the lone forward typically has fairly limited defensive range, whereas the wingers can often have major defensive responsibilities, depending on the flow of the game.

- *Zonal defending or a mix of zone and man?* Here again, the evolution of the game has much to say about the decisions confronting the coach. Thirty years ago, teams played with sweepers (a center back behind the back line) and often man-marked the opposing attackers. Zonal defending has created more sensible, flexible defending systems wherein the team can maintain its shape and more cleanly transition to the attack when the ball is won. Similarly, the use of zonal defending on the back line, along with the change in the back-pass rule in 1992, has encouraged teams to play a higher, more compact line with the incorporation of goalkeepers comfortable playing with their feet. However, many teams still opt to man-mark in special situations wherein a dominant opponent threatens to win the game alone (either directly or through his distribution of the ball) if he does not receive special attention. Therefore, this remains a consideration when designing defending tactics and responsibilities.

- *Defensive balance?* A key consideration that must be consistently addressed is whether the team is in balance without the ball. As the term implies, part of being defensively sound is being able to defend well and aggressively in the space around the ball while also being prepared to thwart threats from other areas of the field, should the opponent be able to change the point of attack. Specifically, as teams look to pressure the ball by running defenders pell-mell at the opponent in possession, it is important to pay attention to what that tactic does to the balance needed in the team defending organization.

- *Where will the team generally try to win back the ball?* Increasingly, teams are trying to win the ball back sooner and further up the field than in previous eras. The realization that winning the ball sooner can often create immediate attacking opportunities or at least disrupt a team's ability to settle into possession has encouraged most teams to adopt a more aggressive, higher-pressure stance in defending. In general, most teams adopt some blend of high and low pressure. For example, a team may try to *counterpress* for the first few seconds (or a set number of passes) after the ball is lost, and if unsuccessful, then drop in to a more conservative, lower pressure posture, trading space for time to consolidate the team's defending shape. Again, the answer to this question must be formulated in rhythm with the team's defending posture. Teams playing three forwards are much more likely to try to win the ball back immediately than those with a single striker based on the fact that more players are already forward to pressure the opponent. Another key factor in this regard is the time in the game and the situation. Many teams will choose to press up high for a set amount of time at the beginning of a game or when they are down a goal to try to gain an advantage. The team must be prepared for all eventualities.

- *How high a defensive line will be employed?* This is a critical question. Every defensive scheme cedes some space on the field to the opposition in an effort to condense the defenders' space, allowing them to defend critical space as a unit. However, some teams choose to drop in and allow the attackers to build up in front of them, making sure there is a tight connection between each of the lines and keeping numbers near their own goal. Other teams want to push their back line up high to condense the space in front of that line, helping their midfield and attacking players to keep pressure and tighten space further from goal. If the team plays a higher line, the understanding between the defenders and the goalkeeper regarding the larger space between them must be sound, and the goalkeeper must assume greater responsibility for controlling balls played in behind the back line.

- *What is the team's specific defending design?* In other words, if the opposing outside back is on the ball at midfield, is the team set up to force the ball inside, where its numbers in the midfield can help win back the ball, or does the team prefer to try to pin the ball to the flank and limit the attackers' options? When the team knows the answers to these questions, and individual players know their roles, then players can be primed to know how to behave in defensive transition.

Marcelo Bielsa. Pep Guardiola said of his Athletic Bilbao team's counterpressing, "They came at us like beasts. I've never played a team who were so aggressive and who denied us so much space."

DEFENDING IN TRANSITION: PRESS VS. COUNTERPRESS

In general terms, *pressing* is the act of organizing the team to win back the ball through deliberate manipulation of the opponents' options in possession. This typically involves an integrated set of principles designed to create a coherent scheme that aims to limit and then snuff out attackers' choices. For example, if a team plays two forwards, the team may set up those forwards to encourage opposing center backs to play to their outside backs. Once this pass has been coaxed and return passes cut off by the movement of the forwards, then the players behind the front line lock down on forward passing options for the outside back, and the ball will often be played in a way that allows the defenders to win back possession.

Counterpressing is different in that it refers to an all-out effort to win back the ball *immediately* after it is lost. This often involves frenzied efforts of players nearest the ball to swamp the player with the ball before their team can get established in possession. More often than not, this concept is expressed in terms of mentality and how it is implemented, rather than specific, position-oriented movements. For instance, a basic counterpressing initiative may involve simply forcing the first opponent in possession to look down through pressure by the nearest member of the defending team, while the team sends as many players as necessary (usually 3-4) in the area to take away all other short options and try to dispossess the attacker. Finally, the team will try as hard as possible to win the ball for three passes or 6 seconds (for example), and if the opponent defeats this pressure, then the team will drop off and defend in its standard pressing scheme.

From the discussion it is clear that the team could both counterpress and press and that these concepts could be complimentary. Some teams choose not to counterpress based on their own characteristics or concerns about their opponents. Others will counterpress only at certain times or with certain cues from their opponents, as it is very physically demanding to counterpress all over the field all the time.

With all this in mind, the many examples that follow give the coach a menu from which to build a coherent, ball-hawking transitional defensive philosophy and strategy.

DEFENDING IN TRANSITION: EXERCISES

Defending has its foundation in 1 vs. 1 situations. Players must be continually drilled in the technical, physical, psychological, and tactical demands of 1 vs. 1 duels. When training players and teams to deal with defensive transition, it is critical to impress upon them the importance of being quick and decisive in applying pressure to the first player to win the ball on the opposing team. It is important to note that depending on the situation and philosophy of the team, this pressure can be to win the ball immediately, or simply to "get his head down," or drive him backward, limiting the player in possession from examining options. This pressure can then be supplemented with additional defenders joining the first defender or filling in underneath as part of the defensive scheme, but it is the first defender (the player nearest the ball when it is lost) who sets the tone by winning back the ball or limiting the attacker's options. The exercises in this chapter are progressive in nature, from individual to group defending, and designed specifically to train players to focus on their defending responsibilities in transition.

In improving our defending, we are making our opponents weaker. –Jurgen Klopp

1 vs. 1 Continuous to End Lines

Play in a 10 × 10 yard grid with an adequate ball supply, with groups of 4-6 players. The duel begins with a turnover, allowing the defender to focus on defensive transition. The attacker attempts to dribble out the defender's end of the grid, while the defender attempts to win back the ball. Play until the ball leaves the grid. After each duel, players change ends and roles.

COACHING POINTS

- Encourage the defender to put the attacker in a corner. There is no reason to give the attacker any advantage. On the contrary, make it tough on the attacker in every possible sense.
- Note that the defender's path to the ball limits the attacker's options (i.e., the attacker should not be able to dribble to his right and the open area of the grid).

- Get in quickly. If the attacker has time for multiple touches in the real game, he can begin to assess his options. The defender must be careful not to overcommit, but he must also force the attacker to worry about protecting the ball.
- Try to get the attacker to turn his back or dribble laterally. Force him away from any direct route to goal.
- Tackle when the opportunity presents itself. A ball dead between the attacker's feet, a long or errant touch all offer the best chance of winning the ball.
- When the ball does turn over, do both players continue to play as they should, transitioning to the next moment? If the attacker then loses the ball, does he transition immediately to defending?

VARIATIONS

- Expand or shrink the size of the grid, depending on the objective (a smaller grid should create more success for the defender).
- Every serve is a throw-in. Now the defender must read the first touch out of the air by the attacker. Can the defender win the ball before the second touch?
- The resting player on each end is a target player for the player trying to score on that end. The attacker can now pass directly out of the grid, eliminating the defender, if the latter fails to angle his run to cut out the pass or apply sufficient pressure.

Manchester City's Nicolas Otamendi cuts out the run of Cristiano Ronaldo of Real Madrid.

1 vs. 1 Continuous: Immediate Pressure

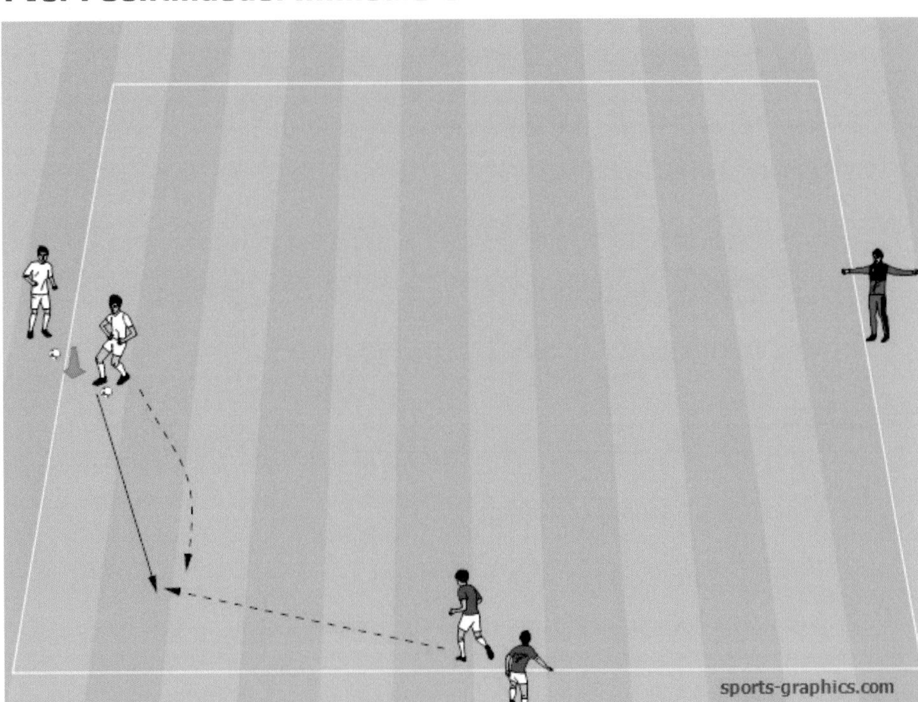

Similar to the first exercise, this setup encourages the defender to immediately get tight with the attacker and cordon him off from the larger grid. Once again, use 10 × 10 yard grids, 4-6 players, and an adequate ball supply. The duel begins with a turnover in the form of a pass from the defender to the attacker. Emphasize the transitional moment. The defender must try to win back the ball and dribble over the opponent's end line. The attacker tries to get out of the corner with the ball and dribble over the defender's end line. Play until the ball leaves the grid. Players change ends after each duel.

COACHING POINTS

- Encourage the defender to put the attacker in a corner. There is no reason to give the attacker any advantage. On the contrary, make it tough on the attacker in every possible sense.
- Note that the defender's path to the ball limits the attacker's options (i.e., the attacker should not be able to dribble to his right and the open area of the grid).

- Get in quickly. If the attacker has time for multiple touches in the real game, he can begin to assess his options. The defender must be careful not to overcommit but he must also force the attacker to worry about protecting the ball.
- Try to get the attacker to turn his back or dribble laterally. Force him away from any direct route to goal.
- Tackle when the opportunity presents itself. A ball dead between the attacker's feet, a long or errant touch all offer the best chance of winning the ball.
- When the ball does turn over, do both players transition to the next moment?

VARIATIONS

- Expand or shrink the size of the grid, depending on the objective (smaller grid should create more success for the defender).
- The defender starts from one knee and rolls the ball to the attacker with his hand. He must now recover his feet and contain the attacker's run.
- Every serve is a throw-in. Now the defender must read the first touch out of the air by the attacker. Can the defender win the ball before the second touch?
- The resting player on each end is a target player for the player trying to score on that end. Note that the player at the defender's line must move to the end of the grid. The attacker can now pass directly out of the grid, eliminating the defender, if the latter fails to angle his run to cut out the pass or apply sufficient pressure.

1 vs. 1 Random Roles

In a 10 × 10 yard grid, two players pass the ball back and forth using one touch. At a signal from the coach, the duel begins, with the player in possession at the time becoming the attacker and the other player being the defender. Both players attempt to win the ball and dribble over their opponent's end line. Play until the ball leaves the grid.

COACHING POINTS

- Because the roles are not assigned before the play begins, both players need to be ready to be the attacker or the defender, which is great training for the transitional moments on match day.
- Which player is sharper in grasping his role at the outset of the duel?

VARIATIONS

- The players head or volley the ball back and forth at the outset until the coach gives the cue for the players to duel. This variation compels players to think in terms of defending a player trying to settle the ball out of the air. Can the defender get tight to the attacker "on his touch," either winning the ball on the next touch or severely limiting the attacker's options?

- The waiting player on each end of the grid becomes a target player. The player in possession can pass to the target player on his attacking end of the grid if he has the opportunity to do so. This rule compels the defending player to think in terms of closing down while also taking away a through-pass that would eliminate him as a defender in the play.

Gerard Pique of Barcelona and Spain separates the attacker from the ball.

1 vs. 1 Recovering Defender

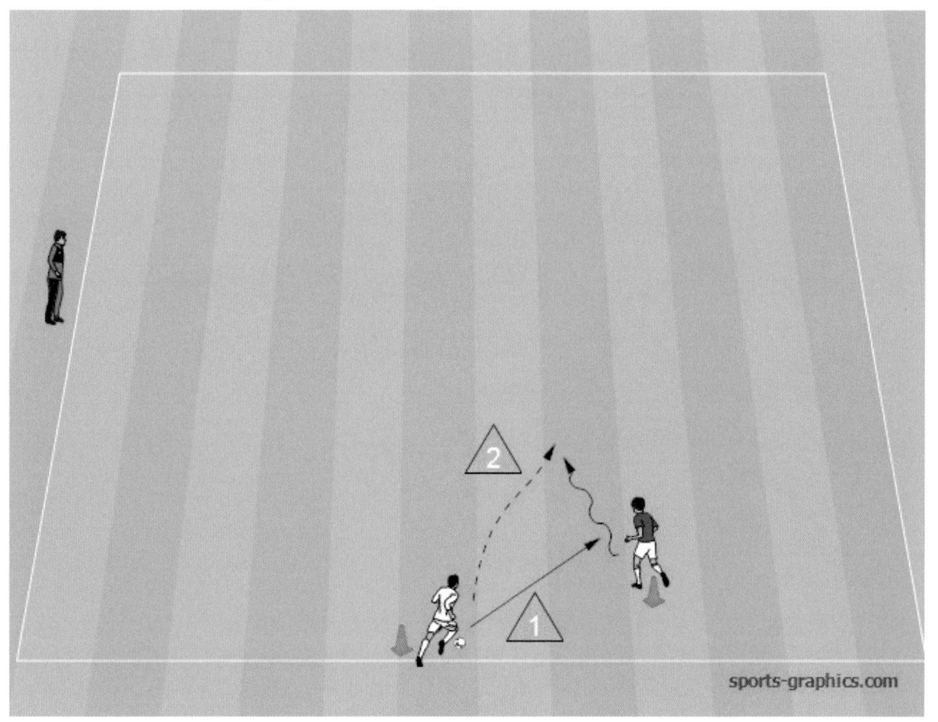

In a 10 × 10 yard grid, the defender should give away the ball and then must recover, getting underneath the ball quickly and attempting to slow down the attacker, or if feasible, winning the ball back and dribbling out the attacker's end of the grid. The attacker attempts to dribble out of the grid over the defender's line to recovery.

COACHING POINTS

- Speed of recognition and recovery. It is mandatory that the defender get underneath the attacker and immediately slow or stop the latter's dribbling run.
- Defend with a physical presence. Particularly if the ball was lost in the front third in the real game, it is desirable that the pressing and recovering player be physical when possible, understanding that in this situation the attacker does not have passing options and so he can be challenged right away.

VARIATION

- Add a server near the defender. The server tosses or volleys the ball to the attacker, and the defender must read the flight of the ball and the touch of the attacker to decide whether to get under the ball or engage the attacker before he can get settled.

Defender Julie Ertz of the United States' National Team, World Cup Champions in 2015

1 vs. 1 plus 1: Press and Recover

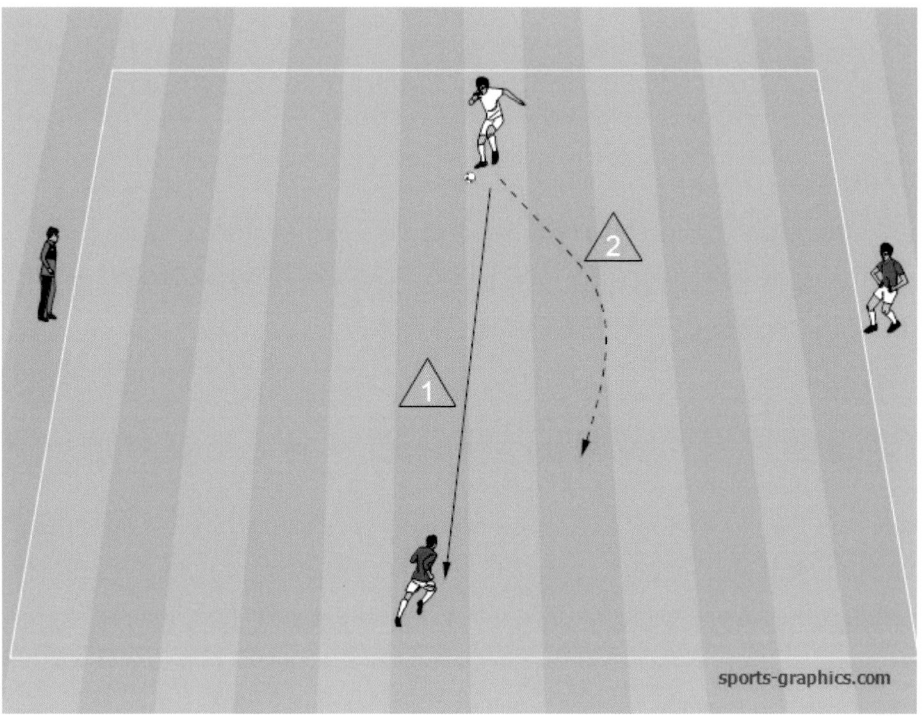

In a 10 × 15 yard grid, the defender passes to the opposite side of the grid to the attacker to initiate the duel. In this environment, the attacker is free to use the extra player (on the perimeter, opposite the coach) to try to combine to beat the defender. The extra player cannot enter the grid and cannot be tackled. For advanced players, limit the extra player to one touch. Note that the attacker is not required to use the extra player. The extra player can move up and down the sideline of the grid.

COACHING POINTS

- To initiate the duel, when the ball is lost, the defender must move to pressure the attacker, while also ensuring that the extra player cannot be used to get the attacker in behind with a wall pass. The defender must learn to bend his run to take away this pass and isolate the attacker.

- If the attacker does manage to play the extra player, the defender must recover to get under the ball and cut out the return pass.
- If the defender does win the ball at any time in the duel, both players must recognize the new transitional moment and continue to battle.

VARIATION

- If the attacker plays the extra player, that player can enter the grid and join play, forcing the defender to deal with two active attackers. Now overlapping runs and other two-person combinations come into play.

FOCUS ON SKILL: DEFENDING FOOTWORK

Dick Bate, the famed FA and FIFA clinician, often gives symposium sessions that focus on the importance of defending footwork. He points out that a massive portion of successful defending is simply getting to the right spot and in good physical form. The vast majority of defending footwork trained in isolation falls under the heading of *jockeying*, which is a critical skill wherein the defender attempts to control the dribbling of the attacker and create a moment to separate him from the ball. Very little attention is given to approach footwork for individual defending. This section presents five defending footwork exercises that, taken together, provide a master class on defending approach footwork and jockeying.

Knee Tag: Getting Focused and Aggressive in the Duel

Players work in pairs. Play for 30 seconds. Players earn one point for every touch they get on their opponent's knees. This exercise forces players into a lower, aggressive stance, which is ideal for individual defending. Talk with the players about the fact that they have to be low and quick and limit the exposure of their own knees (which is good footwork for defending) to be successful. Play several rounds, changing partners after each duel.

Ball Tap: Focus

Players work in pairs with one soccer ball. This exercise requires the defender to work low and focus on the ball. Defenders earn a point each time they touch the ball with their hand(s). Attackers can manipulate the ball with their feet as needed but cannot run away. Duels last for 30 seconds and then players change roles. Periodically, they change partners as well. Encourage the defenders to be physical, without fouling, in their duels and to use good, quick footwork to confuse the attacker and create opportunities to touch the ball.

"If I had to tackle, I had already made a mistake in the duel." –Paola Maldini (left), legendary AC Milan and Italian National Team defender

Defending Approach Footwork: Diamond

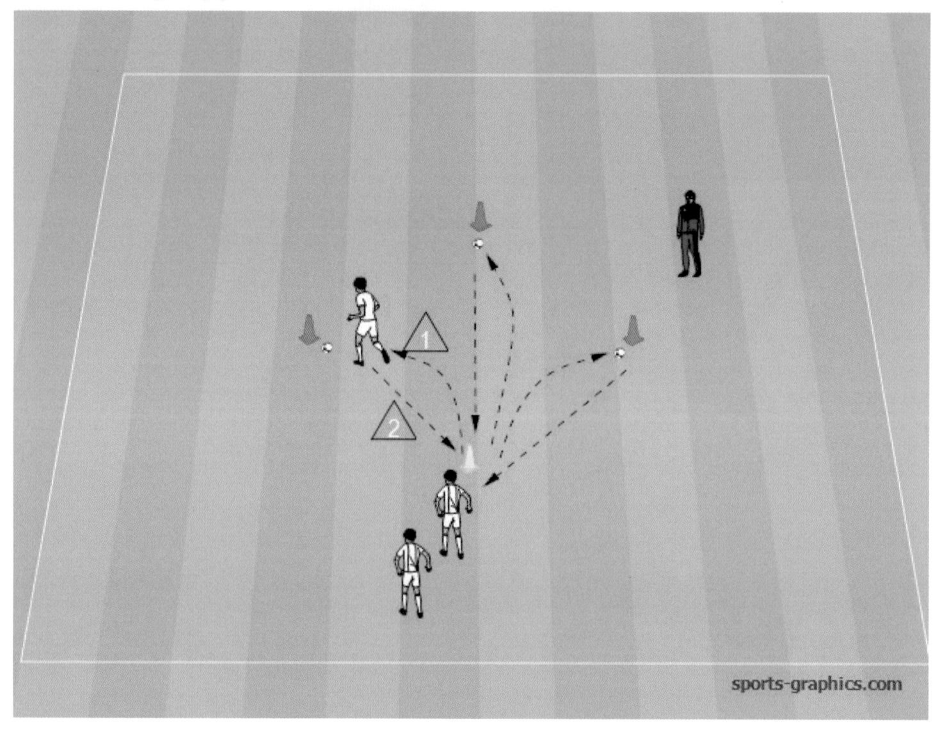

The purpose of this exercise is to isolate the last few steps the defender takes to close down an attacker. The defender starts at the bottom cone (yellow) and approaches the left cone. He then backpedals to the start point before closing down to the center cone. After recovering again, he works to the right-side cone before returning again to the starting point. The focus here is the quality and the speed of the footwork.

COACHING POINTS

- Posture. The defender should approach with legs bent, not crouching but low enough to be able to focus on the ball and make adjustments.
- Steps. The first step or two can be longer to close the ground and then the defender should take short, choppy steps to be able to make adjustments.

- Angle. The defender should show the ball outside at the wide cones and one side or the other at the center cone. To show the ball to a side, the defender bends his run. This action limits the options for the attacker, simplifies the defender's work, and also indicates to supporting players his intention to take away a particular side or option.
- Distance. One of the most common errors in approach work is for the defender to get too tight to the ball. Getting too close will allow the attacker to push the ball in behind the defender and the duel will be lost. Staying too far away will allow the attacker to look up and work without pressure. Every player is different in his defending characteristics, but the idea is to get close enough to get the attacker to look down, but not so close as to overcommit if the immediate intent is to control rather than tackle.
- Set-steps. These are the last couple of steps the defender takes before stopping or changing direction. Many players are not controlled in their feet or throughout their bodies when they make these steps. The defender's weight should be low and equally dispersed between the front and back feet (balanced) and the last steps should be *stuck* (i.e., distinctive, showing that control).

VARIATION

- Replace the three cones with players to make the defender's work more realistic.

Color Cones: Mental and Physical Approach Work

This is a very effective environment for demonstrating the importance of sharpening both the mental and physical dimensions of approach footwork. Four defenders step into the lane from the tall yellow cones, where resting players await their turns. Each group has four differently colored cones. The coach calls out colors, and the players must close down the appropriate color. Emphasize getting low and sharp, quick footwork.

VARIATIONS

- The coach calls "Turn," and the players must change places with the players behind them (shown).
- The coach calls "Switch," and the players must switch places with the players in the cone set at the far end of the grid.
- The coach calls the series of cues more quickly, and sees if the players can continue to make the right moves and display proper technique with the added pressure.

Philipp Lahm (right) of Bayern Munich and Germany closes down Pablo de Blasis of Mainz.

Defending Footwork: Jockeying to Control an Attacker (1)

The purpose of this environment is to help players understand how to control an individual attacker through jockeying. The defender passes the ball to the attacker and then closes down. The defender may not tackle in this exercise. Instead, he tries to slow the attacker's progress through the cone lane through jockeying. On reaching the last red cone, he must dribble at speed through one of the two flag goals. The defender attempts to be the first to get through the gate. Change roles after each repetition.

COACHING POINTS

- Jockeying. The act of controlling the attacker involves closing down, which was highlighted in the first two exercises in this section. Once the defender gets into good position, he controls the attacker by slowing the latter's speed and limiting his dribbling options. To control the attacker's speed, the defender must stay between the attacker and the goal, and he must force the attacker to focus on the ball (look down) rather than on his attacking options. The specific footwork of jockeying involves *chop* steps that allow the defender to establish and maintain the controlling distance between himself and the attacker. The defender's balance, focus (on the ball) and ability to be physical when possible are all factors in good jockeying.

- Winning the duel when the ball is pushed in behind the defender. When the defender has controlled the attacker through the cone lane, he must then win the duel when the ball is pushed in behind him. This crucial moment is simulated in the final stage of the duel (below). When the attacker attempts to get through either flag goal, the defender must use good footwork to turn, get shoulder-ahead to the goal, cut out the attacker's run, and get through the gate before the attacker.

Defending Footwork: Jockeying to Control an Attacker (2)

1 vs. 1 (×2) with Countergoals

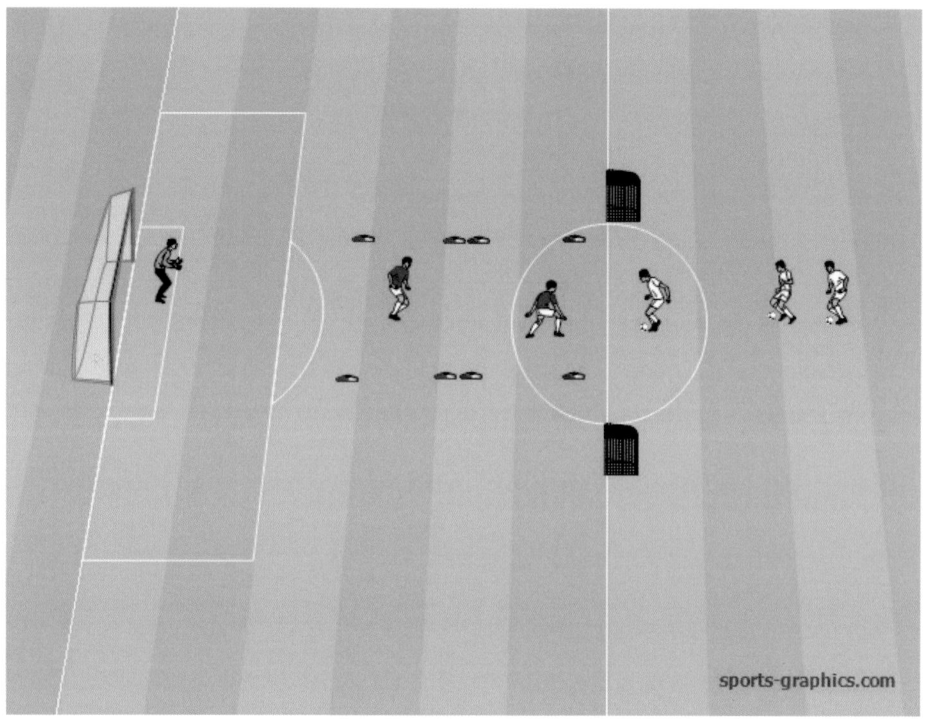

Another variation on the 1 vs. 1 duel, this exercise requires the attacker to win two consecutive encounters before he can go to goal. If the defenders win the ball (they are confined to their respective grids until they win the ball), they both join the play (2 vs. 1) and try to score in either countergoal.

COACHING POINTS

- This exercise has the benefit of demonstrating the importance and rewards of good defending, as the defenders get to push out and try to score if they win the ball. Encourage them to understand the moment of transition when the ball is won and to score quickly on the counter.
- For the attacker, the ability to react to negative transition is an important lesson. The attacker will have almost no chance if he loses the ball and lets down even for a moment, as he cannot cover both goals. His only hope is to immediately engage and isolate the player with the ball and then win it back.

1 vs. 2

Here the defender is immediately presented with an overload situation. After the turnover, he must delay the two attackers and try to drive them away from the cone goal. If the defender wins the ball, he attempts to dribble out the attackers' end line.

COACHING POINTS

- The defender must recognize that he is outnumbered and try to slow the play (give some space to the attackers, keeping them in front of him, until his small goal is threatened.
- The defender should try to keep both attackers and the ball in his vision and in front of him.
- The defender must tackle only when certain to win the ball, understanding that a failed commitment will likely mean a lost duel.
- Are there circumstances when the defender should apply high pressure?

  1. A poor touch that allows the defender to close down the attacker and win the ball.
  2. The opportunity to isolate the first attacker. For example, if the attacker can be trapped in the corner, facing away from the goal and his teammate, then he can be pressured because he is very unlikely to be able to find help out of the predicament.

Second Defender: Base Exercise

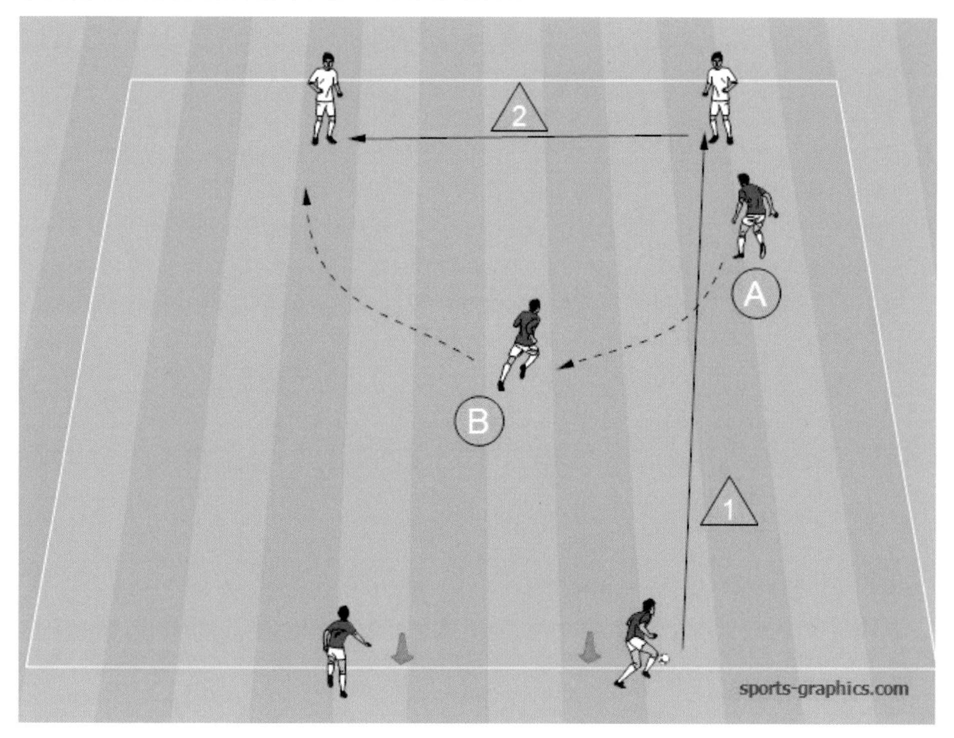

It is critical that all players understand the first and second defender tactical relationship. This exercise is a useful warm-up and refresher for players to rehearse runs and communication together. Each sequence begins with a member of the defending pair passing to an attacker, simulating a turnover (1). The two attackers deliberately pass a ball back and forth (2), otherwise remaining in position. The defenders (A, B), work in pairs and alternate in the first and second defender roles as they move up the field toward the attackers. The orange cone goal is used as a reference point only, and the coach can freeze the exercise to point out that the goal must be covered by the movements of the defenders as they close down. When the defenders reach the attackers, they do not tackle. Rather, they follow the passes back and forth between the attackers until the coach calls for the next pair to enter the area.

COACHING POINTS

- The first defender is the player closest to the ball. He needs to call the ball (by calling "Ball!"
- the defender clarifies his intentions to his teammates and also helps pressurize the first attacker.
- The first defender should get close enough to the ball to apply pressure, while also being aware of the space behind him (the goal in this case) and the position of his partner.
- The other portion of the first defender role is the need to limit the options available to the first attacker. In the diagram, defender A makes a curved run to the ball, forcing the pass to go in the direction of his covering partner (B).
- Note that when roles change, B's run is similar to that made by A, forcing the ball back toward his covering partner. A, meanwhile, comes underneath B, providing cover to his partner and screening the goal.
- The covering defender must also learn to be the eyes of the pairing. His communication ("Left" or "Right") helps the first defender understand where he has cover and organizes the defense.

PROGRESSION

- Place a target attacker between the orange cones. The passing players can try to play to the target if the defending pair fail to screen out the *window* to the attacker.
- Allow the attackers to move laterally and toward goal as the exercise progresses.
- Allow the defenders to tackle and try to dribble out the attackers' end of the grid.

Chile's Alexis Sanchez encounters Argentinian defenders in depth.

2 vs. 2 plus 4

This is an outstanding environment for training and observing the first and second defender roles. Teams play 2 vs. 2 (the active players are in the center of the grid), plus four target players in the corners of the grid. Active players receive from their own color and pass to the corner targets in the opposing color. Note that this is in keeping with our theme, in that a pass to the opposition by a target (or a loss of possession) is the cue for the players to practice the transition to defending. In the example above, the red players have received from their own team and are trying to pass to the white targets in the top corners of the grid. Restarts come from the corners, and there are many opportunities to observe the first and second defending as well as the shifting of those roles. Note that in the opening phases of the exercise, the active players may not pass back to the servers in their defensive corners. This restriction will create more turnovers and therefore more transition. Also, the perimeter players may not pass to one another. Rotate the middle players after 2 minutes.

COACHING POINTS

- How quickly do the players transition with the change of possession?
- How quickly can the defenders sort out their roles (first and second defender) and get to pressuring, covering, and screening out through-passes?
- How well do the defenders communicate? If the players are undisciplined about calling the ball and confirming their cover in this simple environment, they will be even less crisp on the more complex larger games.
- Can the defenders sense the danger of combination play between the attackers (1-2, overlap, etc.)? How would they cut out those combinations?

PROGRESSION

- Players under pressure can play back to the supporting players in their defensive corners. This rule change will allow the attackers to relieve pressure and force the defending pair to adjust to more movement of the ball and shifting of their tactical roles.

Manchester City's David Silva (left) and Raheem Sterling (right) dispossess Southampton's Nathan Redmond.

Huber 3 vs. 3 Continuous to Goal

This is a grueling, outstanding environment for teaching the responsibility for small group defending in front of goal after a turnover. Two teams are organized in groups of three. One team starts on defense and must turn the ball over to its opponents. It then defends its goal. The only way a team switches to offense for the next serve is to win the ball and score on its opponent's goal. If it concedes a goal or defends successfully or stops its opponents and wins the ball but does not score, the next group from the team remains on defense to start. It's very difficult to win the ball and score consistently, and the team defending is often worn out chasing the ball and desperately trying to find a means to turn the game through tackling and counterattacking, which is precisely the goal of the exercise and the mentality to grow in players defending in front of their goal after a turnover.

COACHING POINTS

- Mental toughness. This is not an easy exercise for the defenders. Who will pick up their teammates verbally, physically, and so forth, and also do the tactical problem solving under pressure?

- The use of space by the defending group. Chasing the attackers may open up areas of the field to attackers. Conversely, sitting in will likely lead to dangerous chances from distance for the opponent and also fail to win the initiative.

4 vs. 4 Functioning as 4 vs. 2

Two teams of four in two 10 × 10 grids. The coach serves restarts as shown. When he passes the ball in to one team, the ball is immediately turned over to the team in the other grid. At this cue, two defenders race in to try to win the ball. If the ball is won and possession maintained, the players try to pass back into their own grid, and play continues. If the defenders knock the ball out of the grid, they return to their own grid, and the coach restarts play with a pass into either team.

COACHING POINTS

- This expansion of the defending environment puts the defenders in a setting where they are outnumbered and creates more of a 360-degree challenge, as the four attackers work to keep the ball and wear down defenders.

- How quickly can the defenders win back the ball? Statistically, the defenders are most likely to win the ball in the first two or three passes, before their energy wanes and before the attackers get settled into possession. Thus, hard and coordinated pressure designed to isolate and win the ball must be the goal of the defending duo.

- If the defenders do not win the ball right away, what is their strategy? Often, the defending becomes individual and ragged. Encourage the defenders to stay together and, if they tire, be patient, looking for a poor first touch or a pass that can help the defenders isolate an attacker.

VARIATION

- Turnovers are made in the air. Thus, the coach tosses the ball in, and the receiving team volleys or heads to their opponents to initiate play.

- High-intensity defending. Defending pairs have a time limit (6 seconds) or a pass number limit (3) in which they can win the ball or the possessing team earns a point. This variation creates intensive, brief duels.

Jerome Boateng of FC Bayern Munich and Germany, ball-winner and defender extraordinaire. Boateng was named the German Player of the Year for 2015–2016 and was named to the 2016 UEFA Team of the Year.

4 vs. 2 Pressing in Four Grids

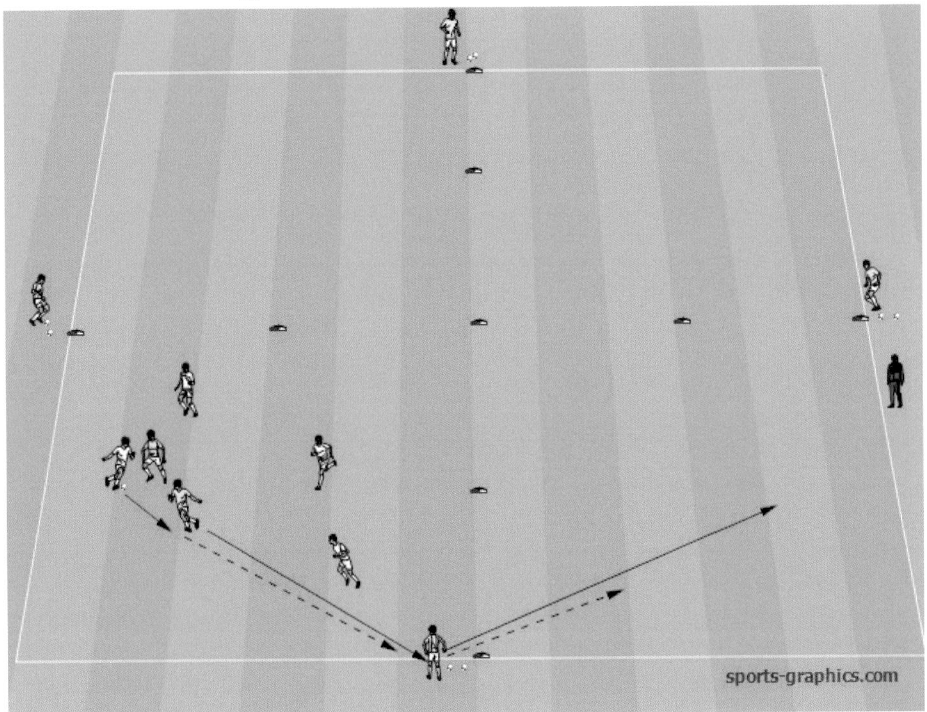

Play 4 vs. 2 for possession in four grids. The attackers need to string together five consecutive passes before they can pass to any of the four targets on the outside of the grid. The targets are waiting defenders who ping the ball into any of the other three grids. The target then joins the defending group, and one of the defenders takes his spot on the perimeter. If the defenders win the ball, they also pass to any of the perimeter targets, who then passes in to an open grid and joins the action. The defender passing the ball to the target takes the new defender's spot on the perimeter. If a ball leaves the active grid, one of the resting perimeter players immediately passes in a new ball and play continues.

COACHING POINTS

- This game creates repeated opportunities for two players to press four attackers. The constant rotation of the defenders assures consistent pressure and also forces defenders to adjust to pairing with a new teammate every few seconds. All this gives coaches adequate time to assess the intensity and the quality of his players' defending. Effort, communication, closing down in tandem, and the ability to win the ball are all on display here.

5 vs. 2 Immediate Pressure

Five players knock a ball (1-touch) in a 10 × 10 yard grid. Periodically, the coach signals for a pair of defenders to enter the grid. The defenders attempt to win the ball and play it out of the grid. The attackers try to maintain possession as long as possible. After the defenders knock the ball out of the grid, they rest at the back of the line, and a new pair of defenders waits to be introduced into the grid at the signal from the coach.

COACHING POINTS

- The defending pair should understand that they will be most energetic during the first few passes, before they begin to tire. Therefore, they need to try to force a mistake with high pressure as soon as they enter the area.
- The defending pair should be coached to recognize cues for them to try to dispossess an attacker. Poor touches, heavy or slow passes, a bouncing ball, a player without good options are all cues for the defenders to try to get in and win the ball.

- Communication (first and second defender roles) between the defending pair is absolutely essential. With the pair being badly outnumbered by the attackers, if the defenders work independently, they are unlikely to win the ball. However, if the pair cooperate in sorting their roles and isolating the ball and an attacker, they have a stronger likelihood of success.

VARIATIONS

- Vary the number of defenders introduced. When the coach signals for the defenders to enter the grid, he also indicates the number of defenders (1, 2, 3). Point out to the defenders, that this is realistic training, as every defending situation is different, and sometimes they may have many teammates available to try to win back the ball, while at other times they may be greatly outnumbered. Talk with the players about the importance of knowing how many defenders are involved (how does that number influence their tactics?).

- For advanced players, play only in the air. The ball is chipped into the grid, and the attackers must maintain the juggle against a single defender. This restriction helps the defender to think through the implications for an outnumbered, single defender. How can he best win back the ball? Depending on the attacker's touch, he may be able to challenge for the ball while the attacker is trying to establish control, or he may need to read touches and try to pick off the aerial pass between attackers. Regardless, this is a useful exercise for teaching how to defend in the air during and after negative transition.

5 vs. 3 (10 vs. 6) Hunting Groups and Transition

Play 10 vs. 6 functioning as 5 vs. 3. The team of ten place five players in each of the end grids, while all six defenders start in the center strip. The coach passes a ball in to either group of attackers, and three defenders enter the grid to try to win the ball. The attackers try to connect six passes for a point. When they achieve six passes, they can try to pass the ball through to their teammates on the other end of the grid. If the defenders win the ball, the center strip temporarily becomes moot, and all players are activated to play 10 vs. 6. The six keep the ball as long as possible. If they get six consecutive passes, they earn a point. When the defenders lose the ball or it leaves the grid, all players go back to their starting positions, and the coach restarts play.

COACHING POINTS

- The groups of three to *hunt* the ball. The groups, though outnumbered, have a good chance to win the ball if they are aggressive and work together to isolate and win the ball. Getting *first* defenders to apply pressure quickly is crucial. The player in possession must be forced to look down and be unable to assess his options. The other defenders have to learn to work off the first defender, taking away the next best options and often intercepting passes. Similarly, the shifting or roles as the ball moves must be crisp and consistent.

- Note that when the attackers connect six passes and go to play into the other grid, defending does not stop. The group of three conceding the point should still try desperately to deny the outlet pass, and the other three defenders in the center strip should screen the lanes out of the attacking grid, trying to steal the outlet pass.

- When the ball is won by the group of six, how do they react? Can they keep the ball for a few passes by moving it quickly and expanding their shape?

- How is the defending transition for the group of ten? This is a very important coaching opportunity. When the ten lose the ball, they should smother the six very quickly, building good negative transition habits.

Four-Zone Group Defending Game (1)

Create two teams of 6-8 players, placing half of each team in alternating zones as shown above. The playing area will vary with the age and ability of the players, but each zone is typically 10 yards deep and 20 to 25 yards wide. When the focus is on defending, it is important to keep the grids tight enough to allow the defenders to get adequate pressure. The coach restarts play from the side of the grid as shown, passing in to any of the four grids. The team in possession attempts to pass to its members in the other grid area, thus connecting an outlet pass and breaking the defenders' press. The defending team can send two players into the grid once the ball is in the area. If the defenders win the ball, they attempt to dribble or pass the ball back to one of their own grids and play continues. Note that if the ball is in one of the central grids, the defending team must send one player from *each* of its grids to defend (see following figure).

Four-Zone Group Defending Game (2): Defending a Central Zone

COACHING POINTS

- Mentality: Defenders must be aggressive and very fast to apply pressure. If they fail to get pressure, they will tire and/or the attackers will find an outlet pass to break their press.
- Can the players in the grid where the ball is lost regain possession before the opponents get out (immediate attacking–defending transition)?
- The role of the first defender. Can the nearest defender to the ball continually apply enough pressure to force the first attacker to look down and not be able to check for outlet options? Can the first defender also make play predictable for the second defender, channeling the first attacker's options?

- Second defender: Are the support positions tight enough, and is the correct angle adopted? Is the communication present?
- Coordination of first and second defender. Given that every situation is different and the play evolves with every movement of the ball, defenders get a lot of opportunities to rehearse communication, angles, and shifting roles to try to isolate the ball.
- Are the defending players remaining in their own zones getting into passing channels to cut out through-passes (see diagram below)?

Four-Zone Group Defending Game (3): Moving to Cut Out Through Passes

COACHING POINTS

- Are the defenders in the far grid (above) assessing the most likely outlet pass and preparing to intervene?

7 vs. 7 Functioning as 5 vs. 5

As the numbers involved expand, so does the tactical complexity of the exercise. Use a 30 × 30 yard grid to emphasize high-pressure defending. This exercise functions well with the numbers shown but is also suitable to numbers as large as 10 vs. 10. Restarts come from the coach (bottom). Teams play to end-line targets. Note that the team starts its defending after a turnover, as the teams receive from their own color and play into the opposing team's targets. In this way, the defensive transition emphasis of the chapter is sustained. Rotate the target players every 2 minutes.

COACHING POINTS

- Defending tactics. The mentality of each group after the ball is lost in open play (or a point is scored) must be to win back the ball immediately through intense pressure. Equally importantly, the coach must also impress upon the defenders the recognition of first and second defender roles (and how they transfer with the movement of the ball and attackers). Communication, taught in the grid exercises above, must be enforced for the group to be successful in winning back the ball.

- As the group tires, there will be possibilities for the attackers to find space and play a long pass into the target players. This is a terrific teaching moment, as the group must recognize its collective responsibility to get the heads of the attackers down (i.e., make them look for short passes to relieve pressure rather than big through-balls that defeat the collective defending bloc).

- What are the team's defending parameters with regard to the use of the boundaries? In this setting, the coach can begin to imprint defending tendencies by encouraging players to use the boundaries to their advantage. Most teams consider the boundary to be another defender, limiting the attacking options of the opponent in possession. Instruct first defenders to drive the man in possession to the boundary and those in covering positions to get underneath the ball and in the lanes available to the attacker.

VARIATIONS

- Passes from target players and service from the coach must be in the air. This variation encourages defenders to read the ball in the air and also the receiving touch of the attacker to see if there is an early moment to close down and win the ball.

- Two-touch minimum for the attackers. Starting the exercise this way (for perhaps 2–3 minutes and then removing the restriction), encourages the defenders to play with aggression and speed, as they will get more tackling opportunities while the attackers try to get in an extra touch.

Striker Thomas Mueller of Bayern Munich (left). Renowned for his goal scoring, he is also a tireless defender. Former Bayern Munich coach Pep Guardiola said of Mueller, "[His] pressing is brutal. If you ask Mueller to make a 40-meter diagonal run to the other wing, he'll do it at full speed, and do it a hundred times more if necessary" (Perarnau, 2014).

7 vs. 7 plus Goalkeepers: Counterpress

Use this environment to distinguish counterpressing in the team's defensive philosophy. Play 7 vs. 7 plus goalkeepers on one half of the field. Each team plays 1-3-2-2. In this game any turnover is followed by an effort to swamp the opponent who has won the ball. Play this game for short periods to emphasize the requirement of increased effort by the entire team in the moment the ball is lost. This game should create somewhat chaotic soccer, as both teams will learn both how to step up their effort and close on the ball when possession is lost *and* also the limits of the chaos that can be tolerated and sustained. In other words, it is clear that the front four (midfielders and forwards) will do most of the pressing, and though the game is played on a smaller field, the players will tire quickly. Additionally, devoting several players to winning back the ball by closing creates inherent risk, as a successful pass or two will likely break the pressure and then the defending team will have to scramble to recover.

COACHING POINTS

- Who counterpresses and where? The coach must decide and choreograph how the team will counterpress. For example, perhaps the team will start by simply counterpressing any time the ball is lost in the front half of the field to an opposing field player. The counterpress will involve both attackers and the closest midfielder, with the other midfielder screening out the nearest pass forward.

- How long to counterpress? Sometimes the press is broken right away, and it is clear that the team will need to drop and condense its shape. Most teams put a limit on the number of passes or time that the team will press. Again, it is usually apparent when a team can no longer sustain the press. Still, the coach needs to talk through the many variables so that the players work in unison.

- The act of counterpressing. There must be relentless effort to pressure the player in possession and cut out his most obvious outlet passes for the counterpress to be effective. Getting tight to the player in possession, being physical with that player, and driving that player to give up possession are all points of emphasis.

- Mentality. Defending is hard work and often the reward is not immediately apparent. Players must buy in to the notion that defending hard for a few seconds may save them minutes of defending as a group by winning back the ball more quickly. They need to fully commit to working together to hunt the ball and demoralize their opponents through continuing to break up their possession.

TACTICAL VIEW: MAXIMIZING THE COUNTERPRESS—SMOTHERING COUNTERATTACK OPTIONS

One of the interesting developments in counterpressing in that last year has been the high-risk/high-reward strategy of thrusting a back line or holding midfield player forward to crush a budding counterattack. Pep Guardiola's Manchester City has proven especially adept at this tactic during the 2017–2018 English Premier League Season. Guardiola's teams at FC Barcelona and Bayern Munich were more renowned for their high-energy defending than their organization on the defensive side of the ball. However, his Manchester City team has added this interesting and subtle variation to their manic counterpressing.

In its essence, the principle is that if the team has begun to counterpress and there is considerable pressure on the ball, and all but one of the forward options for the man in possession are being screened out, and the option is a fairly long pass, then a defender or occasionally a holding midfielder will crash forward to intercept the pass, deny the turn, or at least pressure the player on the ball to concede possession by playing backward.

The sudden, decisive, and surprising arrival of this defender is invariably very destructive to the counterattack being hatched by the opposition and often results in Manchester City launching its own high-speed counterattack when possession is won.

The risks of launching a player from a safety role into an aggressive run forward while the opponent has possession are considerable. If the defender is late, the attacker may get turned and be able to push the ball and the attack forward against a weakened back line. If the attacker is able to win the ball and find a support option, the attack may keep its momentum, and the Manchester City defending shape is weakened.

Balancing these risks, though, is the fact that a few forays forward like this can ruin the belief of the opponents that they can successfully hold the ball, much less counterattack. In addition to the loss of confidence, the counterpressing and related closing of space and time tend to compress the opponent's shape, and the opponent tends to resort to spraying hopeless balls forward to relieve pressure, playing further into the hands of Manchester City's ball-possession-offensive philosophy.

Thus, the idea of running a defending player forward to cut off a predictable outlet pass by the opponent is worth considering in planning the team's counterpressing philosophy.

Fabian Delph of Manchester City erases a Borussia Dortmund counterattack with a timely intervention.

7 vs. 7 plus Goalkeepers: Recovery

This exercise is designed to help the team cope with negative transition when the group is not in a good position to defend. Player 7 vs. 7 plus goalkeepers on two-thirds of a full field. Each team plays 1-3-3-1. When one team scores, two of that team's defenders must sprint to the end line of their attacking goal and around a cone before rejoining play. This action will almost certainly unbalance the team and encourage its opponents to counterattack quickly.

COACHING POINTS

- After a few goals and recovery situations for each team, stop the game and discuss the reasons for the runs by the defenders and the implications for both teams. Help the defending team (after they score) to understand that its midfield players will need to drop in and cover for their backs while they run and recover. The group will need to delay the opponents as much as possible and also try to drive its attack into wide spaces and away from goal.

- Coach the striker from the team recovering to make good decisions about his running. He may be best served by pressuring a back whoever receives an outlet pass from the goalkeeper (if he can force a bad pass forward), or he may be best served to drop in and encourage the back line of the opponent to bring the ball forward slowly. Clearly, much will depend on the situation and the quality of play by the opponent along its back line.

7 plus 1 vs. 7 plus 1 Pressing In-Depth Zones Game (1)

This environment is used to teach players to defend together over the different levels of the team. Play 7 vs. 7 plus each team having a target player beyond its opponents' end line. Each team plays three defenders, three midfielders, and two forwards, all confined to horizontal zones that divide the area into thirds. The goal from an attacking point of view is to pass the ball into the feet of the target player beyond the end line. The targets can move back and forth but cannot enter the field and cannot be tackled. The targets are on one touch and must play to the opposing defenders when they receive. Restarts come from the coach at the bottom of the grid.

COACHING POINTS

- Begin with a walk-through demonstrating the above scenario. The two forwards for each team must create *funnels* through which the ball will be played forward by the opposition. The funnel could be formed around any of the opponents' defenders, and it cannot be passive. In other words, once the ball is isolated at the top of a funnel, the attackers must close down on the defender and try to win the ball.

- As the funnel is being created, note the behavior of the defending team's midfielders in the central zone. Because it is clear that the ball will have to be played into their funnel, the players in the funnel can lock down on their opponents. The far-white player is screening out a difficult pass to the far-red midfielder while also shading toward the likely pass in case he can double down on the near red-midfielder. The near-white midfielder sees the pass being made to the near-white midfielder and once the pass is released, he has placed himself even with the target of the pass, preparing to step in and win the ball.

- Finally, note that the white defenders have also tightened up on the red forwards and shaded their movement toward the center, knowing that the pass is likely to come into this area through the funnel.

- Take a moment to emphasize the value of the work of the forwards. They may not win the ball, but if they do their jobs and are tireless in creating funnels, the work of the players underneath will be clarified and rewarded, and the forwards can know that they have helped win back the ball.

- Similarly, note that if the midfielders and defenders relax and do not tighten down on their opponents in the funnel, the work of the forwards is wasted, and they are lost to the defending block as the play moves forward. All have a role to play in pressing and winning back the ball.

- Note that all the funnel concepts are subject to the preferences of the coach as to where the ball is to be shown (inside or outside or some combination).

Ajax players close down and strip Schalke's Guido Burgstaller in UEFA Europa League play in 2017.

7 plus 1 vs. 7 plus 1 Pressing In-Depth Zones Game (2): Side Funnel

Here the attacking team has the ball on the wing, and its back is being closed down and funneled by the white-team forwards. As before, the near-white-team midfielder is getting tight to the near-red midfielder, and the other white-team midfielder is in a position to screen a pass to the other red midfielder. In the back zone, the white-team defender in the funnel is tight to his attacker, while the central defender is splitting his attention between the other forward and the target player. The third back is closing the gap, knowing that the ball will likely be played forward into the funnel.

Netherlands and Liverpool defender Virgil van Dijk gets tight to Luxembourg attacker Maxime Chanot.

7 plus 1 vs. 7 plus 1 Pressing In-Depth Zones Game (3): Central Midfield Funnel

This slide shows how the same ideas apply when the ball is played forward and the midfielders for the defending team have not been able to prevent the opposition receiving the ball and turning, defeating the defensive work of the front-runners. The midfielders still squeeze the player in possession and try to force his pass to a predictable target, who is tightly marked by the back-line players. Note here that the funnel also works in reverse, as the front-runners for white are doing their utmost to limit the back-passing options for the midfield opponent by screening passes to the wide defenders. If the man in possession opts to play back, he will likely need to play centrally, and the funnel will be reapplied when the front-runners are able to close down.

Holm Functional Pressing in the Front Third: 5 vs. 5 plus Targets (1)

Play 5 vs. 5 on a field as wide as the 18-yard box, with the target team attacking the goal and playing with three front-runners and two midfielders. The group defending the goal fields a goalkeeper, three backs, and two midfielders, as well as a pair of targets just across the midfield stripe and outside the center circle, as shown. The coach has a supply of balls in the center circle.

Use this environment to help the front-runners and supporting midfielders understand the use of shape and pressure to destroy an opponent's possession coming out of their back third.

The team defending the goal is given possession with every restart from the coach, but the pressing group is live on the first touch of the ball. The team defending the goal tries to play outlet passes to its targets at midfield, while the pressing group works to isolate and win the ball. Here the coach can imprint priorities and tendencies for this group, from where to funnel and win the ball to triggers for pressing. When the pressing team wins the ball, it goes to goal. To focus the activity, limit the pressing team to 10 seconds or four passes to score before another restart.

Holm Functional Pressing in the Front Third: 5 vs. 5 plus Targets (2): Throw-In Restarts

VARIATION

- Mix in targeted restarts that can be used as triggers for pressing. Throw-ins (above), goalkeeper distribution, required aerial receiving of the service from the coach, and so forth, can all be useful training cues.

Functional Pressing: 8 vs. 8 plus Goalkeepers

This exercise evolves the team's pressing into a functional game. Two teams of eight plus goalkeepers play a standard game on three-fourths of the field. One team plays 1-4-3-1, while the target (pressing) team plays 1-2-3-3, allowing teams that play a three-man midfield and three-man front line or some derivative of 4-3-3 (e.g., 4-2-3-1) to work with full forward line and midfield units. Similarly, the team it plays against (white above) plays a four-man back line and three-man midfield, so the practice should imitate match numbers everywhere but in the back for the target team and, perhaps up top for the other group. It is useful to put limits on the time the target group possesses so that the bulk of its effort is expended in defending. Accordingly, one can limit the number of passes the yellow team can connect before scoring or similarly allow only a few seconds before possession is returned to the white team. Restarts come from the coach, who passes in to the yellow team. Yellow must turn over the ball on the first touch, playing long to white (simulating a turnover) and triggering the team's pressing.

COACHING POINTS

- The team's pressing priorities. Will the team counterpress in some or all circumstances? If so, for how long and in what parts of the field? What is the posture (i.e., the line of confrontation) when the counterpress does not win back the ball? What are the triggers for pressing? Possession by an outside back? A backward pass to the back line?
- Who calls out or signals to press? With many teams, the press is activated by a player clamping down on an opponent under certain conditions. In other cases, the coach gives a cue.
- What is the approximate line of confrontation? This will vary by team and often by match conditions or the opponent, but having a general sense of where the ball is to be challenged and won will add cohesion to the press.
- What are the responsibilities of each player with the movement of the ball? Does the team wish to push the ball to the flank or force play through numbers in the center?
- How long will the team press? Sometimes this is demarcated by a certain number of passes or seconds, and at other times (i.e., when the team is trailing late in the match), it may be that the press is continuous.

Celia Sasic (6) leads the charge as the French National Team presses and wins the ball against Germany.

THE ANATOMY OF PRESSING—CHOREOGRAPHING A TEAM PRESS AFTER THE LOSS OF POSSESSION

Italian National Team head coach Cesare Prandelli organizes his team.

When a team has rehearsed all the components of team defending, from 1 vs. 1 duels through group defending and pressing activities, then the coach can consider implementing coordinated *team* pressing as a means of response to negative transition. As outlined at the beginning of the chapter, there are numerous variables for the coach to consider in contemplating pressing, from the talents and needs of the team, to the abilities of the opponent and match situation, and each team's pressing will vary based on those factors. The other key consideration is how the team will *transition*. Specifically, if the team wants to press, what is the moment(s) when pressing or *gegenpressing* will be applied? Most often, there are cues from the opponent and the game that can trigger the press. The following pages present an example of how a team might design and implement a simple team pressing strategy.

Team System of Play: 1-4-2-3-1

The first point of consideration is the team's system of play and style. The team mentioned previously utilizes a 1-4-2-3-1 system. Today, this is a very common formation, and in and of itself, it does not commit the team to a particular type of defending because players can be deployed in a number of ways within the system to either play with more emphasis on pressing or a more conservative posture.

Team Attacking Shape: Front Third

The team's attacking posture is very aggressive, with both outside backs bombing forward, trying to get to the end line. The team's center backs and one or both holding midfielders form the defending bloc when the ball is turned over.

POSSESSION IS LOST: *GEGENPRESSING* OR COUNTERPRESSING

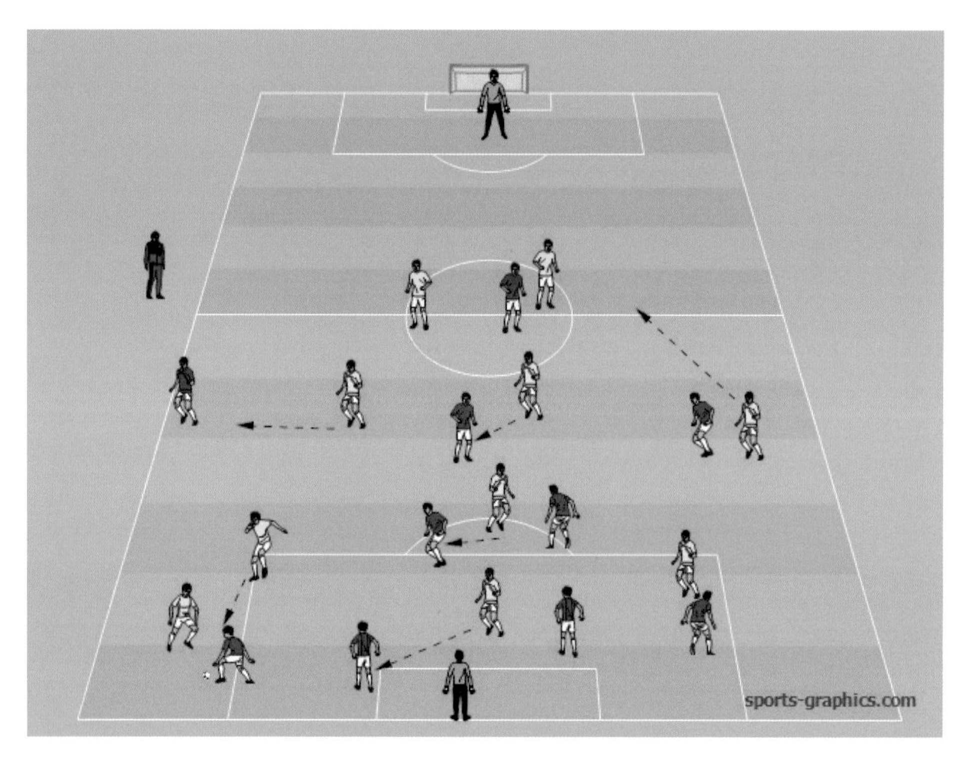

Over the past decade, the concept of *gegenpressing* or counterpressing has become a pillar of team defending for many high-level sides. In *gegenpressing*, the team's priority when losing the ball is to win it back as soon and as high up the pitch as possible. Therefore, if the ball is lost in the front half of the field with members of the team in close proximity, there will be an all-out effort by those nearest to the ball to close down and tackle the opponent in possession.

It's noteworthy that pressing can be a complex undertaking and that there are many variations. Some teams press based on the ball only, running people to the vicinity. Others press with an emphasis on opponents, covering up available help to the man in possession. Finally, still others press based on passing options, trying to pick off the most likely pass. Indeed, many pressing schemes involve some blending of these variants.

For the purposes of this book, a sample pressing philosophy, a blend of man-oriented and pass-oriented pressing will be highlighted. In the diagram above, the right back has lost the ball near the end line to the opponents' left back. The right forward moves quickly with the right back to try to win the ball. The center forward, attacking midfielder and the holding midfielders all move to screen out the most likely outlet passes for the player in possession. The consequent lack of options is called a *shadow*, or an area near the man on the ball where no options exist. The idea then is to apply immense pressure for up to 6 seconds or three passes to determine whether the ball can be won right away.

Manchester City rallies to the ball against Real Madrid.

AC Milan's Nigel de Jong (right), an extraordinary screening player, wins the ball against Fiorentina.

Designate a *Screening* Player

Part of the tactical planning in designing a team-pressing concept is the idea of designating a screening player. This player is responsible for cutting out dribbling runs and passes forward by opponents in crucial space during and after negative transition. The idea here is that the team identifies a player who has sharp ball-winning abilities and who has the physical grit to win balls in dueling situations. This role can be shared by many players (i.e., whoever happens to be in the right position when the ball is lost), or the role can be more narrowly defined and performed by one or two players. Nigel de Jong, pictured above, who plays for AC Milan and the Netherlands, is a prototypical holding central midfielder: tough, physical, a proven ball-winner whose mere presence inspires his team on defense and also forces opponents to consider alternative attacking strategies rather than playing through his space.

Pressure is broken. If the team is unable to win the ball and the opponents establish possession (holding the ball for the preset time or number of passes), the team drops off and tightens its shape.

Here, the opponents release pressure by passing to the goalkeeper. As no member of the defending team is in a position to pressurize the goalkeeper, the team starts to drop off, conceding space for time to condense its shape. Note that there will be times (i.e., when the team is trailing late in the match) when the center forward or another player will be detailed to go alone and press the goalkeeper to force the opponent to play forward.

Restraining Line

The team may adopt a restraining line to help the players focus on winning the ball at a particular point on the field. Teams that choose to play low pressure in particular often adopt restraining lines as rallying points, and it's important to note that there will be times when the line may not be particularly useful (e.g., when a number of players are caught forward or the opponent chooses to play directly and plays deep into the front third from distance). However, the use of a restraining line, as shown above, is that the team can condense behind the chosen point and then attack efforts to push beyond that point, hopefully frustrating the opponent. The idea here is to present a cohesive defending shape that is poised to win back the ball. When the team is established in its defending shape, the coach can then set cues for resetting the press.

How do restraining lines and pressing schemes mesh? A team may recover to a restraining line when the press is broken or if the situation dictates that the team does not want to press beyond a certain distance from its own goal (e.g., if the team has a lead or is tired, or is playing against a team that appears likely to break any press applied near its goal). The point here is that the line of confrontation can be wherever the ball is lost, or it can be preset to help condense the team shape or provide a rallying point if the first effort to press is broken.

Trigger 1: Pass to Outside Back

Many teams use a *trigger* to coordinate the activation of team pressing. For example, when the opponent (above) passes to either outside back in possession, the whole team pushes forward, compressing the space available to the attackers and attempting to force a pass that can be intercepted. Note that the left forward (highlighted in the circle) forces the ball away from the touchline. This is a matter of choice for the coach. Driving the pass to the center means more options must be covered, but also channels the ball to where the bulk of the defenders are located.

Trigger 2: Backward Pass From Opponent Midfield

Another useful trigger for team pressing is a backward pass. While the ball travels away from the team's goal, the team has an opportunity to shrink the space available to the opponent by pushing forward as a group. Thus, the back line pushes forward, the midfielders tighten their marking of their opponents, and the front line push forward as well, with the wing forwards seeking to prevent a pass to either outside back and the center forward looking to split and isolate the two center backs.

Other useful triggers can be a poorly weighted (slow) pass or a poor touch in this area of the field (near the restraining line), or a pass to a particular player (e.g., the holding midfielder, if he's facing his own goal or side-on).

Trigger 3: Pass to Holding Midfielder Who Receives Facing His Own Goal

This is a very common pass in most systems, and a pressing move from this trigger is designed to upset the opponents' comfort and momentum on the ball. The idea here is to prevent a turn in possession from the holding midfielder, who then has a wide range of options. The United States Men's National Team under Bruce Arena (2017) used this trigger with good success against CONCACAF opponents in World Cup qualifying that year. As with all pressing moves, in the best-case scenario, the attacking midfielder can perhaps intercept the pass in to the opponent or tackle and dispossess him. Alternatively, if the player safely receives the ball but is forced to play backward, he and his teammates are now aware of the new pressure, and their passing movement has to begin again, farther from goal. Meanwhile, the defending team can push higher up the field, further reducing time and space for the opponent.

Trigger 4: Poor Touch by Opponent in the Middle-Third

In this case, the press is unleashed by the center forward, who recognizes a long uncontrolled touch by the opposing center back. The center forward decides that he can arrive at the ball at or near the same time as his opponent. His teammates recognize his move and join in the pressing action.

THE GOALKEEPER AND NEGATIVE TRANSITION

Marc-Andre ter Stegen of Germany and FC Barcelona organizes the German defense in transition.

In a book dedicated in part to a goalkeeper coaching legend (Tony DiCicco) and written by a pair of goalkeeping specialists, we would be remiss if we did not address the role of the goalkeeper in negative (and later positive) transition. It is easy to neglect the goalkeeper in many aspects of team training, and transition is no exception. At first blush, one would simply want the goalkeeper to get or remain "home" when the ball is lost to his team.

However, the goalkeeper has the best view of the game from his perspective in behind the team, and he must be adept at assessing threats and organizing the defense as the play develops. In this sense, the goalkeeper must be attuned to the entire defensive and negative transition philosophy of the coach so that he can implement and enforce those ideas in the run of play. Similarly, the goalkeeper's working relationship with the back line must be seamless in orchestrating defensive transition.

In addition, the trend is definitively in the direction of the goalkeeper having radically expanded duties controlling the space in behind the defense, which is an area opponents will always probe in attempting to counterattack.

Given that any negative transition strategy requires the goalkeeper's organization and participation, it is useful to include here sample training environments that facilitate the incorporation of the goalkeeper in the defensive transitional concept.

Goalkeeper Gianluigi Donnarumma of AC Milan clears the ball against Sampdoria.

4 vs. 5: Back Line and Goalkeeper Defending Through-Passes (1)

In this exercise, the coach can work with the back line and the goalkeeper to defend the space between them. The server (right, in blue) restarts play by pinging a ball into any of the four white players, who begin at or near their cones. The defender with the ball passes to any attacker (simulating a turnover) who then pushes it in behind the defenders' line. The goalkeeper and the backs attempt to get on the ball first and clear it, trying to play back to the blue server at the far end of the circle. If the attackers get on the ball first or prevent the clearance, they attack the goal. Encourage the attackers to vary the location of their through-pass, as well the type of pass (lofted, driven, ground pass, etc.)

COACHING POINTS

- The goalkeeper must take control of these situations where a ball is served behind the retreating back line. Will he come out and clear or control the ball, or must the backs run down the ball? If the backs do get the ball, are they playing a back pass to the goalkeeper, or trying to clear it themselves? Quick, correct decisions must be made. Standard communication must be imprinted and given at the proper time. Good technical execution of the clearance must also be expected of the goalkeeper and backline players.

VARIATIONS

- Periodically, the coach can serve a ball in from the side angle, simulating an early cross, to restart play. The retreating back line often find this one of the most difficult balls to deal with and the ball moves across the goalkeeper's vision, making it harder for him to judge and parry or clear.

4 vs. 5: Back Line and Goalkeeper Defending Through-Passes (2)

The previous exercise is altered, with service from the deep player, who simply chips balls over the top of the back line for the goalkeeper and defenders to sort out. Adjust the starting position and numbers of the attackers to create suitable pressure. Again, the defenders and the goalkeeper try to play back to the server, whereas the attackers try to play to goal.

COACHING POINTS

- The coach can work with the goalkeeper and the back line to establish height and priorities for their lines. Because the serve timing is so predictable, there is a static start, allowing the coach and defenders to measure their ability to handle the ball floated or driven in behind. How high can the goalkeeper start? How well do the backs deal with the space in behind them against live competition? Do you want the team to utilize an offsides trap? If so, this setup is useful to imprint shape and gives cues to step up or drop. It may be useful to try a few dry runs, with just the defenders and the goalkeeper and to map out back passes, clearances, and cover.

6 vs. 7: Back Line and Goalkeeper Defending Through-Passes (3)

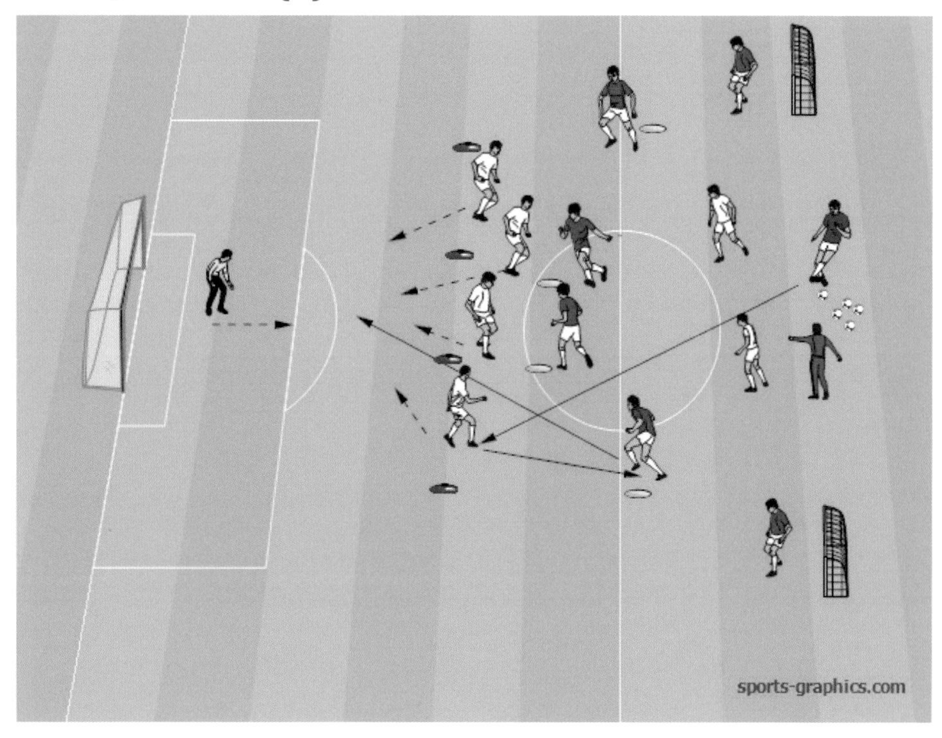

VARIATIONS

- Add countergoals and a target player(s) for the defending team, as well as a pair of defenders for the attackers. Continue play once the defenders or goalkeeper have the ball to set patterns for positive transition. Note that the defenders guarding the small goals may not cross over the midfield stripe.

11 vs. 11: Goalkeeper and Back Line Dealing With Balls in Behind

Play a standard practice game with the groups playing the team's regular formation (here 1-4-2-1-3). At a cue from the coach, the ball is turned over and then played in behind the opposing back line by the team gaining possession. This condition creates numerous, quick through-balls, forcing the back line and the goalkeeper to sort out their roles and work together to control dangerous space.

COACHING POINTS

- Starting positions. As the coach can call the turnover while the ball is anywhere in the middle or attacking thirds for each team, is the goalkeeper in good position to work with the back line in particular in negative transition?
- Communication. The exchanges between the goalkeeper and the back line must be standardized, crisp, and early to allow both the field players and the goalkeeper to play at pace and with intent. The goalkeeper must learn to be decisive and understand that the call is his to make. If he wants to deal with the ball, he must let the back line know by calling "Keeper!," and if he wants the backline players to deal with the through-ball, he must typically let them know ("Away!") and then drop off to be available for a back pass.
- Coordination. If the goalkeeper will deal with the ball, where do the backs run to? For example, it is usually good practice to urge one center back to run past the goalkeeper to provide depth and cover in case of a poor touch or blocked clearance. Whereas the wide backs often track wide once the goalkeeper gets the ball to be available as distribution targets.

VARIATIONS

- Require a particular type or location for the through-pass (e.g., lofted ball behind the center backs) to focus on dealing with a specific threat.
- Limit the goalkeeper's options for distribution—for example, he must use his nonpreferred foot, or he cannot use his hands even in the box to force him to deal with whatever is thrown in behind with the rest of his body and his feet in particular.
- Compel the goalkeeper to stay in his 18-yard box, and all through-balls should be played back for back passes to rehearse this critical exchange.

Chapter 4

THE TEAM IS ABOUT TO WIN THE BALL

You play soccer with your head. You just use your legs to run.
–Johan Cruyff

The effort to maximize the team's effectiveness in counterattacking must address the players' ability to understand the entire process of transition. Again, traditional tactical training emphasizes that the break begins when the ball is won. However, it seems apparent that further benefits can be gained by training players to understand that anticipating and planning for the interception of the ball can allow the team to win the ball earlier and more often and also break more effectively on the counterattack.

In the continuum of analysis that runs from (1) pressing the ball to (2) preparing to win the ball, and then (3) winning the ball, to finally (4) counterattacking, there will inevitably be overlap, and this study will address the bulk of the process in the chapter on counterattacking. However, it is useful to look at some of the crucial advantages accrued by training the team to think in terms of *preparing to win the ball* through recognition of the moments when *the team is about to win the ball.*

There are essentially two components in preparing to win the ball. First, the team can be organized to win the ball earlier and with an eye toward what to do when the break is on. Secondly, the team can be trained to anticipate the moment of the turnover, gaining even a few seconds on its counterattack through earlier and faster mental and physical transition.

For example, consider the following:

- The opposing right back has made a long run to his attacking end line, and he loops in a lazy cross that will be easily fielded by the goalkeeper. If the attackers on the team about to win possession recognize the potential for a counterattack from the impending positive transition, the goalkeeper may be able to distribute long to one of his strikers, particularly in the space vacated by the opposing right back, before the opposition can adequately recover.
- The opposing center back has played a long ball on the ground toward the team's back line, which will clearly win the ball because it outnumbers the opponent in this instance 4:1, and that lone player is nowhere near the ball. As a consequence, the entire midfield group for the defending team begins to move toward a more spread out attacking posture. The resulting few steps may give the receiving team a much better chance to counterattack because its shape will be adjusted before the opponent organizes to defend.

Chapter 3 dealt in detail with the team's response to the loss of possession, from small group to team-wide defending through pressing schemes. The important message in this chapter is to connect those efforts with the actual winning of the ball. Once players and the team are organized to press opponents and win back the ball, it is necessary to then prepare them to anticipate the winning of the ball and prepare to counterattack.

6 vs. 6 plus 1 plus Goalkeepers: Recognizing That the Ball Will Be Won

This is the same setup utilized in chapter II, utilizing a small-sided game to help players read and react to likely changes of possession. Two teams of six deploy in 1-2-3-1 tactical arrangements with a neutral defender who plays near the middle of the field. When the neutral defender wins the ball, he passes immediately to the team that had been defending, then changes teams to defend again. Encourage the two teams to play fairly directly and to attack. The addition of the extra defender should create somewhat choppy soccer that features a fair number of changes of possession. Play a regular game without corner kicks. The goalkeepers play a ball in right away if the ball is played over an end line.

COACHING POINTS

- As with the imminent loss of possession, this exercise is looking for evidence that players can recognize and react to the likely winning of the ball by their team. After a few minutes of open play, stop the action and talk with the players about cues they might see that would tell them the ball may be won by their team. Long passes, poor touches, situations where the player in possession is closed down and has few or no options, and so forth, should all be pointed out.

- Use three phases to draw out increased recognition and earlier, coordinated reaction by your players. First, require that players on the defending team briefly raise a hand in the run of play when they think their team might win the ball. Stop play on several occasions for both teams and have the players talk about what they saw as they raised their hands (or failed to raise their hands).

- When the players are clearly recognizing the imminent winning of possession through individual means, switch to a verbal cue to be used by each team. For example, the white team can call out "White!" when its members think they will win the ball. This group recognition is a valuable tool for getting players on the same page in transition. If all players see and point out the likely winning of possession, then they can begin to think in terms of a quick switch to attack when the ball is actually won.

- In the final stage, help the players work through a group *reaction* to the recognition of the possible winning of the ball. The teams must continue to call out verbally the possible change of possession. Additionally, talk with the players and seek examples of how they can shift faster to an attack posture. For instance, in the diagram on the previous page, it is clear that the white team will win the ball through the neutral defender, who is going to cut out the pass in to the forward. The white forward recognizes this development and alters his run slightly to be available for an outlet pass. Not every turnover will produce such clear-cut examples, but some instances will, and if we help players see the possibilities associated with rapid, coordinated transition, we help our team play faster.

Michael Bradley of the United States intercepts a pass in a friendly against Germany in 2015.

Uber den Fluss (Over the River): Finding the Outlet Pass When the Ball Is Won

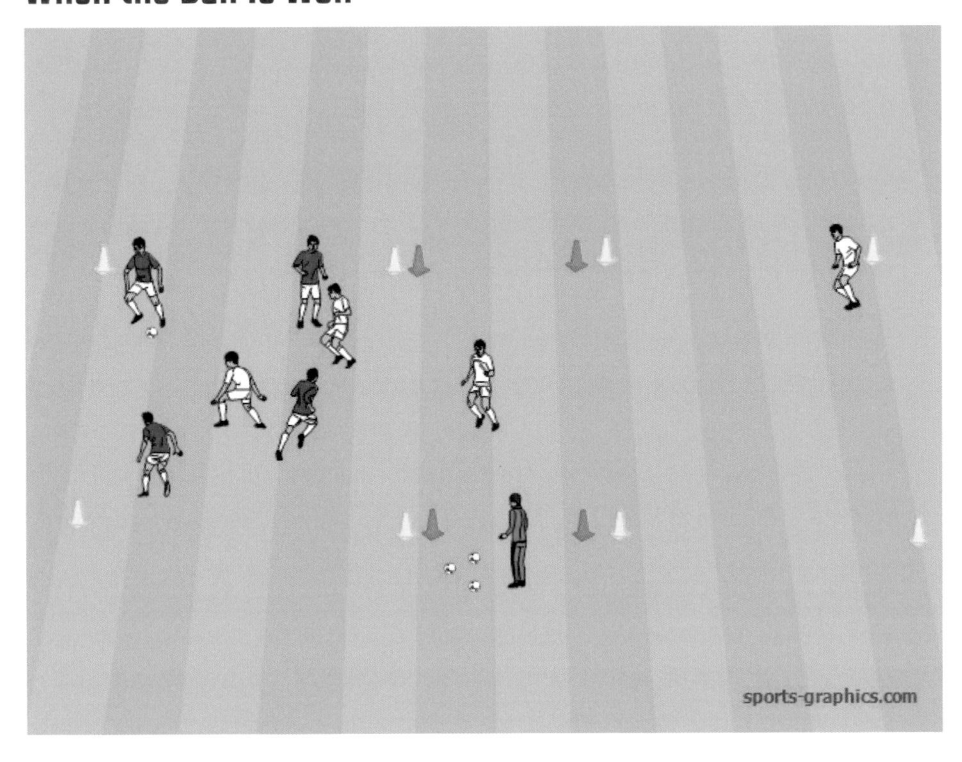

This is the perfect exercise to demonstrate the anticipation of winning possession and the thought process once the ball is won. With two teams of four in two grids plus a narrow central zone, the coach restarts play with a pass to either team in their home zone. The focus here is on the defending team, which sends two players into the far grid to win the ball. An additional player goes to the *river* or central grid, and one player remains behind in the home grid. When the defenders win the ball, they must pass to the player on the river, who in turn passes to the player left behind in the team's home grid. Alternatively, if the player on the river is put under pressure right away by an aggressive defender, he can set the ball for a recovering teammate to pass or dribble into the *home* zone.

COACHING POINTS

- First and second defender roles. Can the defenders win the ball before the attackers get settled and the defenders tire? The two defenders must work to isolate the ball and pounce on poor touches or vulnerable passes.

- The exit ball. This pass is critical to transitional moments as the team prepares to earn possession. The defenders must understand that as soon as they win the ball, they will be swamped in a 2 vs. 4 situation, so they must win the ball with an eye toward playing the outlet pass before they can be dispossessed.

- The target player. The outlet player must be active, constantly looking to find the right angle for the pass even before the ball is won. He should also receive *side-on*, which is to say half-turned in the direction he intends to play. Finally, this player should learn to decide whether it is better to turn (no pressure) or set the ball (lay it off for a teammate to play or dribble forward if the target player is under pressure).

- Finally, the resting player must also think in terms of where he wants to receive the pass when the ball is won. He will likely want to be as far away from the other team as possible to give his team time to join him and solidify possession, but he may want to push into a corner or be on the middle of the line (and continually adjust), depending on where the pressure will likely first arrive.

VARIATION

- Add a defender in the river (center zone) to challenge the outlet pass. This addition puts much onus on the outlet player to be more active and subtle in his movement.

- Require that the outlet pass be made to the player in the far (home) grid and travel over the river (center grid) in the air. That player must then play first time to the player in the center grid before the team can return to its grid and solidify possession.

Poachers: Intercepting Passes and Transitioning to Counterattack

Play 4 vs. 6 in a grid with four corner countergoals. The coach plays all restarts from the edge of the grid. The team of six places one player on each side of the perimeter of the grid. These players are limited to two touches and cannot be tackled. The other two players from that team are free to roam the grid and also have a two-touch limit. Their team simply tries to keep possession. The team of four is free to move about in the grid. Its focus is to intercept passes and then score through any of the four corner countergoals.

COACHING POINTS

- The group of four must learn to intercept passes through early movement, pressure, coordination, and reading play. The opposition's touch limits will create frequent opportunities for the group of four to win the ball.
- The first pass is important because the ball must not be lost immediately after it is won. The use of four goals should allow the group of four to experience success in transition.

VARIATION

- One-touch limit for the players on the perimeter to apply even more pressure to the opposition group.

Chapter 5

THE TEAM WINS THE BALL

THE RECIPE: INGREDIENTS FOR EFFECTIVE COUNTERATTACKING

Given the prominence of counterattacking in tactical planning today, it is worthwhile to consider the basic elements of the movements, with the caveat that some elements may not be present every time on the break. These principles should be known to the players and continually emphasized by coaches to ensure maximum coordination.

Recognition

As the previous chapter outlined, the moment of recognition must precede the winning of the ball. Players must anticipate the turnover and transition to be able to fully exploit consequential openings during the transition.

Transition to Possession

This is the moment that the ball is won in the run of play.

Assessment

Both the ball-winner and his teammates must quickly assess whether a fast counterattacking move is possible or if the team will need to consolidate possession. There are many factors that influence this decision.

- The makeup and posture of one's team. If the team likes to play forward and possess considerable athleticism, the coach may be more inclined toward counterattacking than a less speedy team that prefers a gradual buildup when possession is won.
- Pressure. If the ball-winner is hard pressed, it will be difficult to get out on the break without first breaking pressure.
- Match situation. If the team is leading and satisfied with the score line, it may be more profitable to slow play and drain the match time. On the contrary, if the team trails late in the match, it may be necessary to risk an attempt to break even if some of the preconditions are absent (i.e., if there is pressure on the ball-winner).
- Opponent. Some opponents are better situated to defend counterattacking than others due to their personnel or tactics. A speedy team that likes to defend deep may be very hard to catch on the break, whereas a less athletic team that defends up high may offer much space for direct counterattacking.
- Defenders' dispositions. Is the other team vulnerable at the moment? If one or more of its backline players are caught out, there may be very good space available from which to counterattack.
- Opportunity. Is the team well positioned to play forward when the ball is won? If the center forward has dropped in to help win the ball in the midfield, there may be limited options for outlet passes to start the break.

Mobility

One of the most critical elements in counterattacking is the ability to change the point of the attack without disrupting the speed of the break. This ranges from an outlet pass (i.e., distribution from the goalkeeper to a striker) to a change of field (e.g., a wing player cuts the ball back inside and plays a ball into space for the wing on the other side of the field).

Speed

Along with mobility, the successful counter typically features speed throughout the movement, as both the player on the ball and those supporting the attack push (often the length of the field) toward the opposing goal. Indeed, one of the most critical elements involved in defending counterattacks is *breaking the speed* of the movement.

Numbers

With rare exceptions, counterattacking moves involve multiple attacking players who provide width and, especially, *options* with which the team can swamp the opponents' efforts to contain the break. This is an important consideration in the system a coach chooses for the team: How many players will be expected to get out on the break, and how many can the team afford to push forward when the ball is won?

Determination

The best counterattacking teams drive their breaks to the opponent's goal through hard running, intelligent passing, *and* determination. It is almost always easier to back out of the counter and settle for possession and a patient buildup, but the most effective counterattacking teams recognize that they must push on if there is any way to push the attack to the goal before the opponent can settle in on defense.

Intelligence and Decision-Making

Although it sounds contrary to the element of determination (above), teams must also recognize whether the counter has failed to unbalance their opponents and be willing, if the way to goal is closed off, to settle in and attempt to break down the opponents through buildup and possession.

Reasons a rapid counterattack, once started, can fizzle:

- The opponent acquires sufficient numbers and balance to stifle rapid forward progress.
- The attacking team lacks sufficient numbers in attack.
- The ball is played to an area (e.g., a corner) where momentum is lost.
- Poor passes (e.g., back foot, overhit, underhit, etc.).
- Poor touches, particularly receiving touches that derail the attack.
- Decisions that break the momentum of the attack (e.g., an attacker dribbles into a group of defenders and keeps possession but is forced into a shielding position).

RECOGNIZING THE MOMENT AND CUES

Recognizing the Moment: Pairs Training to Start the Counterattack

When the ball is won, there is a critical moment where possession must be consolidated and the group must decide which counterattacking strategy holds the most promise. The essence of the decision is the assessment of whether there is pressure on the ball. If there is pressure, teammates must rally to the ball and give options to defeat the opponents' pressing. If there is no pressure on the ball, the player in possession must look up and assess whether a long passing option that gives a chance at goal can safely be contemplated. This exercise is an outstanding introduction to the concept of turning over an opponent and the steps to consolidation of possession and counterattacking. Introduce each of the three options before explaining (just before phase 5) how they relate to the game and counterattacking.

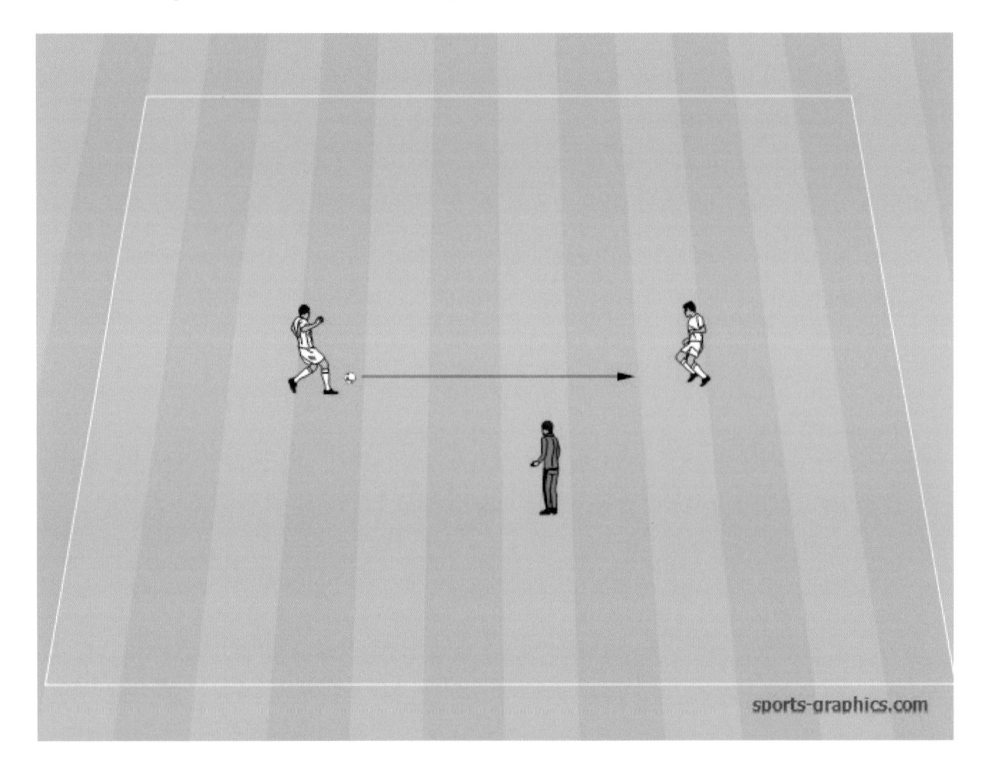

Phase 1: Pairs passing. Players knock the ball back and forth, remaining approximately 10 yards apart.

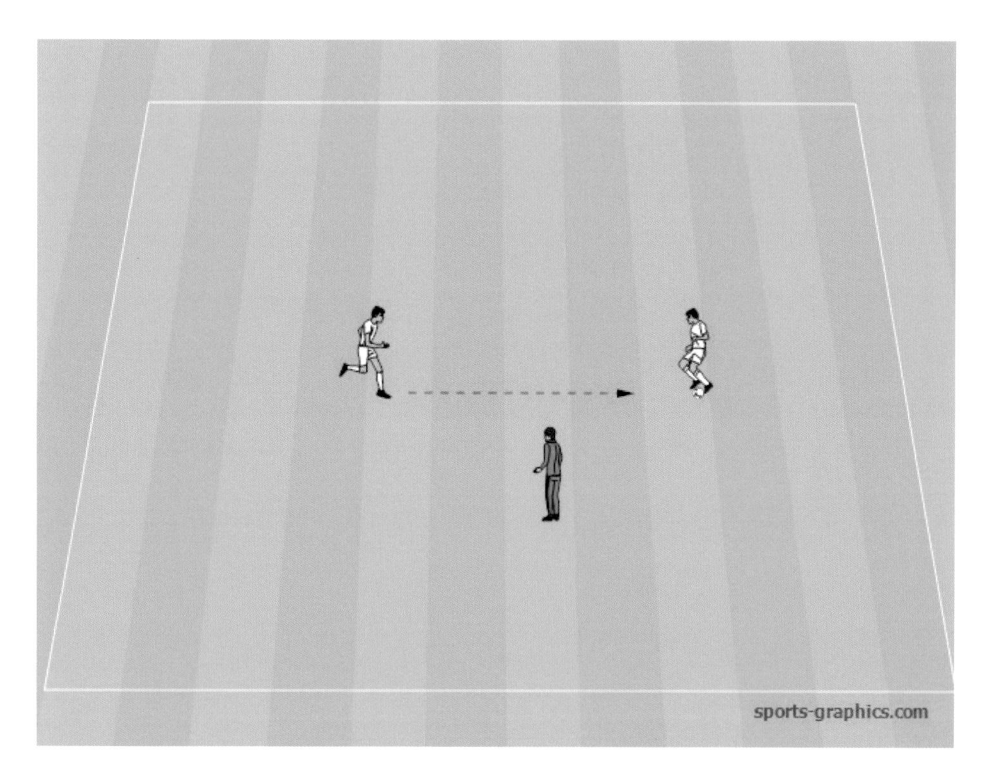

Phase 2: Pairs passing with immediate support cue. Once the players have had a chance to warm up, bring them in and explain that there will be three options added and that they need to rehearse each option. First, every 4-5 passes, the receiving player steps on the ball and looks down. At this cue, his partner must sprint to the ball and take over. When the supporting player arrives, the player on the ball jogs to his partner's starting position and play continues. Ask the players what the focus on the ball is meant to signify. Explain that the purpose is to simulate pressure on the player in possession, in which case his partner must sprint to his aid.

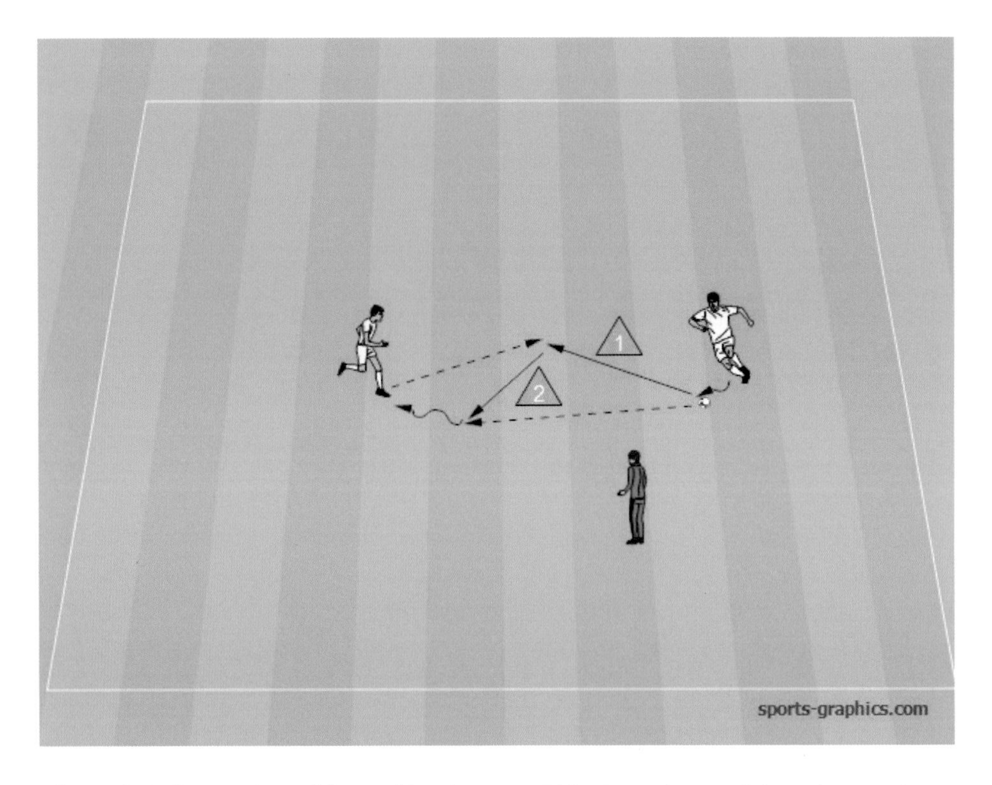

Phase 3: Pairs passing with combination cue. This time, the receiving player takes a short touch to the side and then looks down. His partner then moves opposite the ball and closer to this partner, who plays a 1-2, and the players change starting positions and play continues.

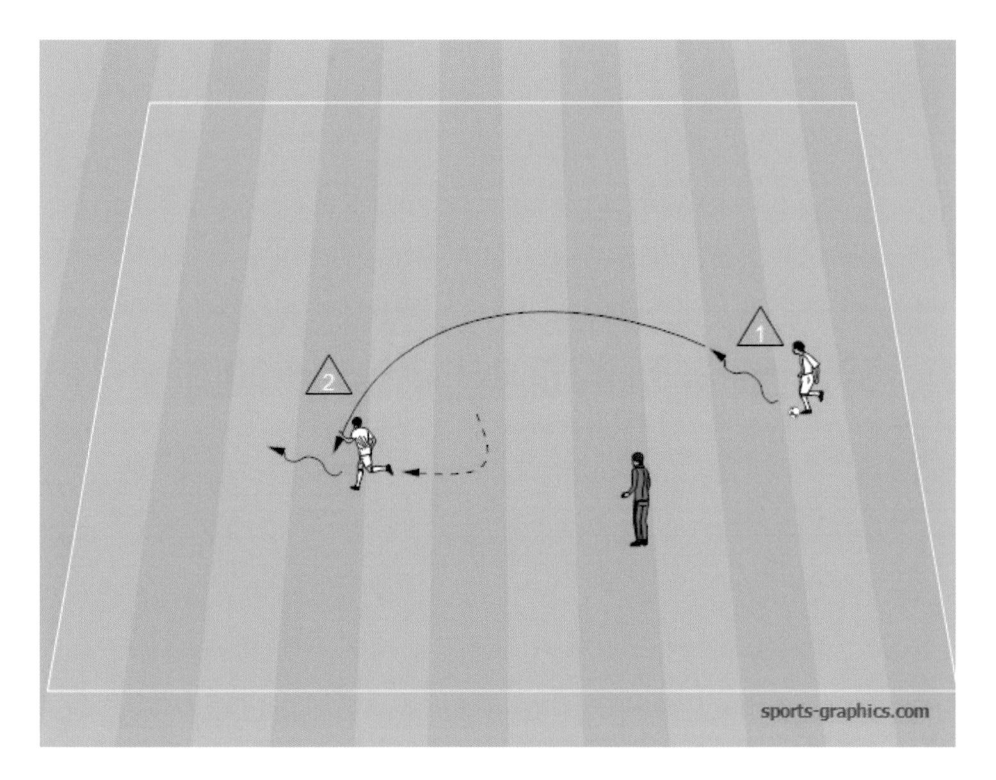

Phase 4: Pairs passing with penetrating run cue. The receiving player occasionally takes a long touch to one side and looks up, prompting his partner to spin off and make a penetrating run forward. His partner plays him into space, then follows his pass, and the pair resume passing in new space.

Phase 5: Pairs passing with varied cues. Once the players have mastered the three options, call them in and discuss each option.

1. When the player steps on the ball and looks down, what in the game is simulated? The cue here is that the ball is won, but that the receiving player has had to go into a protective posture, focusing on the ball. His team must rally to the ball to be available to help release pressure (therefore the run to the ball).
2. The player tapping the ball to the side and looking down is also under pressure. By moving to the ball, the supporting player presents himself to combine and break the opponents' pressure.

3. The long touch and look up indicate that there is no pressure on the ball. Therefore, the other player spins off and gets forward into space, where a ball is played for him to run onto.

Together, these options give the team cues and scenarios to rehearse for the moment possession is won, helping facilitate successful counterattacking. Send players back to work on all three options this time, with them reading the cues from their partners.

1 vs. 1 Continuous: Timed Duels to Pressure Attacker

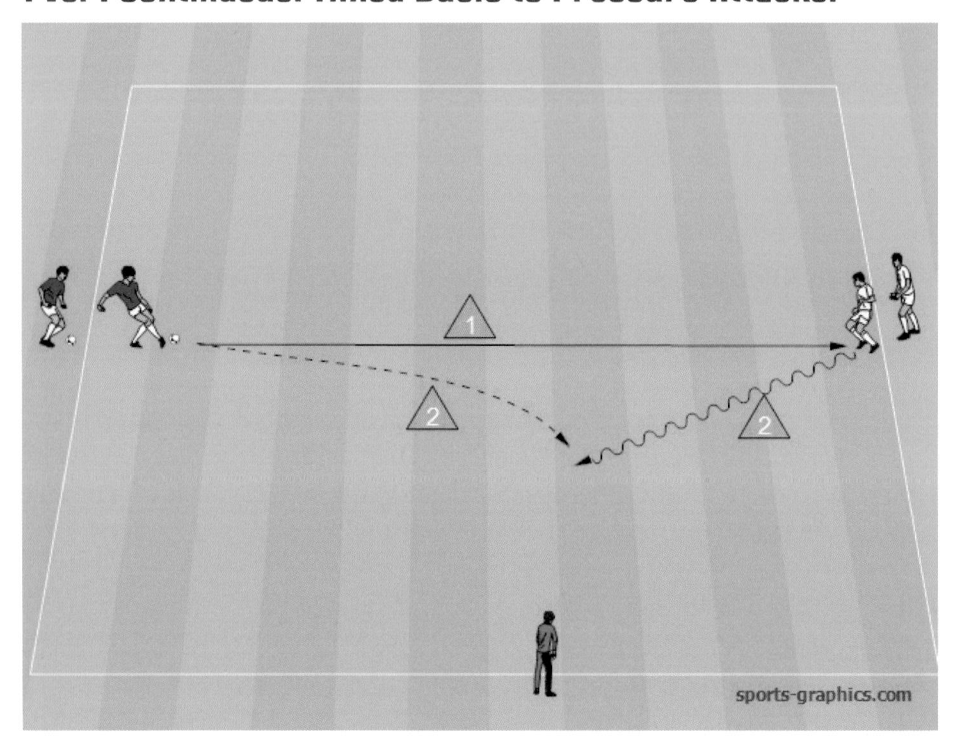

Here the most basic form of transition (1 vs. 1) is rehearsed with the focus on the attacking role. Play in 10 × 10 yard grids. Players win the duel by dribbling over their opponent's end line. All duels start with a pass (a turnover). The coach times each duel, allowing 5 seconds from the first touch of the attacker for the duel to be completed. In this environment, there is pressure on the attacker to defeat the lone defender and get out of the grid before the defense, in theory, can be organized. Players change ends after each duel.

COACHING POINTS

- Players must understand that time is critical after a turnover. For the attacking roles, which are the focus here, the emphasis is upon breaking down the defender before he can get settled and before help can arrive. Therefore, a quality first touch and rapid dribbling to space, as well as the ability to break down the defender on the dribble, are critical to the attacker's approach.

- After several minutes of play, stop the action and ask the players where this situation could occur on the field. Players should understand that one should not run at a defender inside one's own 18-yard box, or even in the back one-third. That said, if the ball is won in this fashion in the front one-third (for instance off an errant pass by an opposing back), the midfielder or attacker winning the ball should and indeed must break down the lone defender if there is no better option (i.e., another player making a penetrating run to goal). Thus, players must understand the situation and when they have license to take on a player in transition.

VARIATION

- The serve from the defender is a throw-in. The attacker must get the ball settled and into space while also expediting the attack.

Lionel Messi vs. Borussia Monchengladbach

Remember that there is no solution for players who break down a defense on their own.
–Anson Dorrance

---

1 vs. 1 From Transitional Pass With Graduated Defending (1)

This is a useful warm-up environment that also compels players to think about their 1 vs. 1 attacking in transition. The large grid above is divided into two equal grids. Each group places players on the end lines and also a single player in the center area. The player with the ball at the bottom of the grid initiates the sequence by touching the ball sharply left or right. The player in the center of the area reads the touch and checks at an opposite angle to receive the pass. This subtle requirement compels players to form good habits about giving good angles from which to receive a forward pass, which will aid in positive transition. The player in the center area then turns and passes into the waiting player at the top of the grid, as shown in the right-side group.

1 vs. 1 From Transitional Pass With Graduated Defending (2)

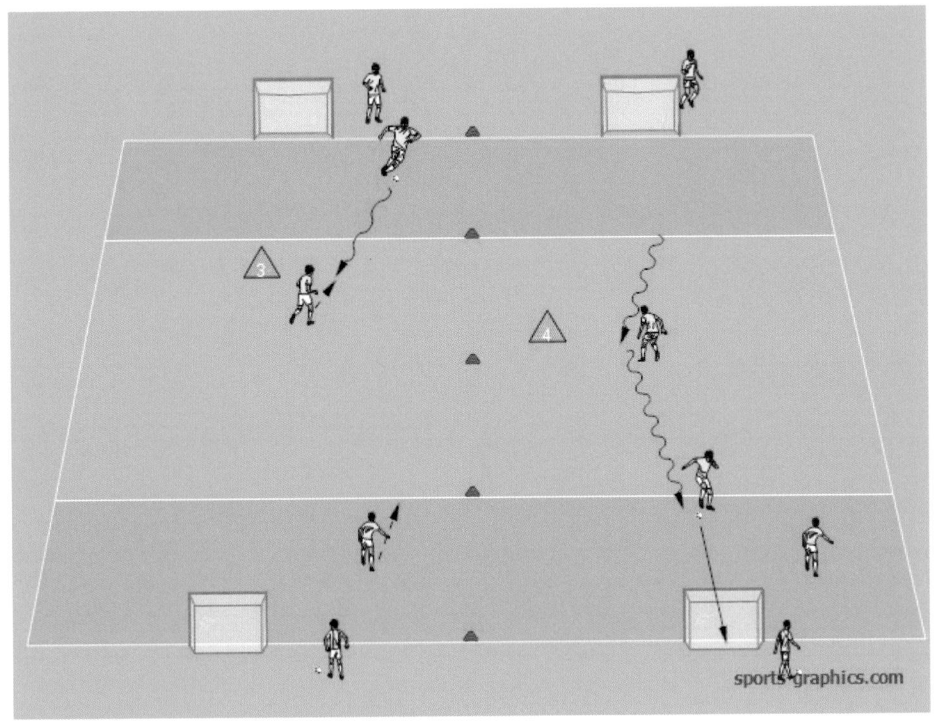

When the player at the top of the grid receives the ball, he thinks in terms of beating one defender to score. He must dribble into the middle area of the grid, where he beats the defender (left and right, above) and then dribbles into the bottom of the grid before he finishes into the small goal. Players rotate from the bottom to the top of the grid and then back to the beginning and the exercise continues. If the exercise is used as a warm-up, it is useful to gradually increase the effort of the defender from passive resistance to medium pressure and then finally to live play.

VARIATIONS

- Use the passive defender to work on the attacker's individual moves (e.g., drag-and-go, scissors, changes of speed, etc.).
- Keep the player who initiates the action in the bottom zone, where he becomes a defender whom also the attacker must defeat (thus, two consecutive 1 vs. 1 duels) before he can finish.

Pressure Finishing: 1 vs. Goalkeeper With 1 Recovering

This is an efficient and telling exercise regarding players' ability to drive the goal and finish. Set up two lines 30 and 35 yards from goal as shown. The defenders start at the more distant line, with the attackers at the closer line. The defender turns the ball over, passing it to the front foot of the attacker, who then sprints to goal and tries to finish. The defender tries to catch and stop the attacker. The defender recovers the ball, and the two players jog back up the outside of the field, changing lines for the next duel.

COACHING POINTS

- The speed of the attacker. His first touch must put the ball into space, and he must sprint forward.
- Do not allow the attacker to pull the ball back. The attacker has the advantage and must go to goal as quickly as possible.
- Teach the attacker to get his body between the ball and the recovering defender. The defender should not be able to get to the side of the attacker and push him off the ball.

- The angle of the attacker's run. Players have a marked tendency to run off at angles to the goal, weakening their shooting angle, and helping the goalkeeper manage the situation. This also allows the recovering defender to gain a better angle to pressurize or tackle the attacker.
- The attacker should not shoot from distance. This is another tendency of young players when they sense pressure. Use this environment to teach the attacker to close to within 7–14 yards before finishing. If the goalkeeper remains near his line, the finishing should be from very close, passing the ball into the goal. If the goalkeeper comes to challenge the attacker, the latter should try to catch the keeper moving and push the ball by him before he can get close enough to block the attacker's effort.

VARIATION

- Turnovers from the defender are tossed in front of the attacker. The attacker must get the ball settled while also accelerating to stay ahead of the recovering defender.
- Move the starting points to different angles and distances.

Carli Lloyd of the United States. Her decisive forward runs and finishing made her the dominant player and Golden Ball Award Winner at the 2015 FIFA Women's World Cup.

1 vs. 1 to Goal: Individual Counterattacking

Continuing the theme of developing the simplest of counterattacks, this exercise pits a single attacker against a lone defender near the top of the 18-yard box. The active defender starts near the cone, 6 yards from his goal. The attackers start from a gate 30 yards from goal. The defender serves the ball, turning it over, to the attacker, who has 5 seconds to score. The defender must sprint to challenge the attacker and confront him as high up the field as possible, and the attacker can either finish from distance or get in behind the defender and try to score.

COACHING POINTS

- The attacker should move to receive the ball as soon as possible.
- The quality of the attacker's first touch. With the defender closing from more than 20 yards distance, the first touch should be positive (toward goal) and a bit longer than normal, allowing the attacker to start running before gathering the ball to duel.

- Approach to goal. The tendency in this exercise with young players is to run off at angles to avoid the pressure of the defender. Unfortunately, this behavior allows the defender and goalkeeper to be more successful, as the attacker works progressively to bad angles and long shooting distances. The attacker has limited time and must take on the defender and penetrate to goal.

VARIATIONS

- Change the serve and approach angles and distances to challenge players on both sides of the ball.
- All serves (turnovers) must be played in the air to the attacker. This variation requires more technical prowess from the attackers as they corral the ball and prepare to take on the defender.
- Incentivize the attacker to shoot from a distance by giving an extra point for goals from outside of the area. Although penetration is more likely to produce goals (and should be emphasized first), allowing the attacker to finish from distance puts pressure on the defender and goalkeeper and allows the attacker to vary his approach.

Christian Pulisic of Borussia Dortmund and the United States: speed and decisive dribbling make him the most exciting American player of his generation.

Numbers Up: 2 vs. 1 Penetrate to Goal

This exercise helps players make good decisions in numbers-up situations entering the final third. The coach passes to player A, simulating a turnover. Player A passes to either player B or C. The recipient of the pass joins A in attacking the goal, while the other player becomes the defender. For this exercise to work efficiently, players must work to quickly fill in the open cones after each attack. Since the roles are not predefined for B or C, encourage players to just push forward from the line and fill the open cones immediately, not concerning themselves with whether they get to attack or defend. If the defender wins the ball, the duel ends.

COACHING POINTS

- Speed of play. Once the pass from A is played to B or C and the roles are clear, the attackers must recognize their numbers-up situation and attack the goal at speed. This exercise should not result in crossing situations.

- Two-person combinations. The use of 1-2s, double passes, and overlapping runs should be encouraged, as these simple combinations make it very difficult for the defender to deny penetration and slow play.

- Change channels. Although the attackers must work directly to goal and avoid balls to the corners to evade the defender's pressure, they must also recognize that changing channels through somewhat wider runs will create better passing angles and frustrate the defender's efforts to keep between the ball and the goal. The caveat here is that the width of the attackers cannot allow the defender to isolate the first attacker.

VARIATION

- Place a time limit on the duel—that is, 6 seconds to score. This restriction adds pressure to the attackers to drive the goal.

- Add a transition reward for the defender, who passes to the coach if he wins the ball.

Speed is mandatory to success. –Pep Guardiola

Numbers Up: 2 vs. 1 plus Recovering Defender

This environment forces the attacking pair to play quickly or lose their numbers-up advantage. Once again, the coach passes to player A to simulate a turnover and initiate each sequence. A and B try to beat C and attack the goal. Meanwhile, player D begins his recovery run with the pass from the coach to A. If C or D win the ball, the duel ends. It is best to divide the team into two groups and have one group play the attacking roles for 5 minutes while the other group defends and then swap roles.

COACHING POINTS

- Speed of play. The attackers are punished for slow play to goal by the imminent arrival of the recovering defender.
- Attack the single defender. Player A should make defender C focus on his attack by running at him and challenging him.

- Player B, the second attacker, must create off player A's run. Can he set up a 1-2? An overlap? Can he run wide and create an angle for a run directly to goal?

- Stay onside. One of the worst practice habits is to simply run to an offside position in this situation, a habit that will thwart the team's counterattacks and create frustration on match day. Encourage players to use width and intelligent running to time their penetration and remain onside.

VARIATION

- Serves from the coach to player A are in the air. A positive, aggressive first touch will be required to maintain the attackers' numerical advantage.

- Vary the starting position and service position to provide different looks for the players.

It's not enough to have the ball. You have to know what to do with it. –Johan Cruyff

3 vs. 2 Continuous Attacking Transition

This is an excellent environment for introducing overload counterattacking (i.e., situations where the attackers have a numerical advantage), from playing a target player to driving the goal. Utilize two teams of five players plus goalkeepers. With each restart, one defender from the previous duel remains on the field as the new target player who receives a pass from the resting pair to initiate the counterattack. Similarly, the last attacker to touch the ball in each duel jogs back to his resting teammates. In this way, a continuous run of 3 vs. 2 duels is sustained.

COACHING POINTS

- The speed of transition from defending to attacking. The start-up pass from the resting duo must be sharp and the target player must work into space right away to receive and start the attack.

- The running from the new attacking players. The tendency is for the players to run straight up field. Encourage them to be quick but also creative, changing channels and speeds as needed to unbalance the defense.

- The use of combinations to overload and isolate defenders. 1-2s and overlapping runs in particular can create difficulties for the defenders and should be a constant part of the attacking tactics.
- Driving the goal. When a player has an open look at goal, that player must drive the goal and finish. This approach will build aggressive, simple, and efficient counterattacking tendencies.

Bumpers Small-Sided Game: Go to Goal

Play 5 vs. 5 plus goalkeepers on an area roughly double the size of the 18-yard box. Each team places two bumpers on its attacking end line. These players are limited to one touch and cannot be tackled. The two teams play 3 vs. 3 plus goalkeepers. To score, the teams must pass to one of their bumpers and then score first time off the bumper's service (see above). Rotate the bumpers every 3 minutes.

COACHING POINTS

- Forward mobility in the attack. This setup requires direct passing into the bumpers and then hard running to goal is rewarded through service. Players should get accustomed to thinking about playing the penetrating pass early and then getting out quickly on the break.
- Touch and time-in-possession restrictions for the active players to discourage dribbling.

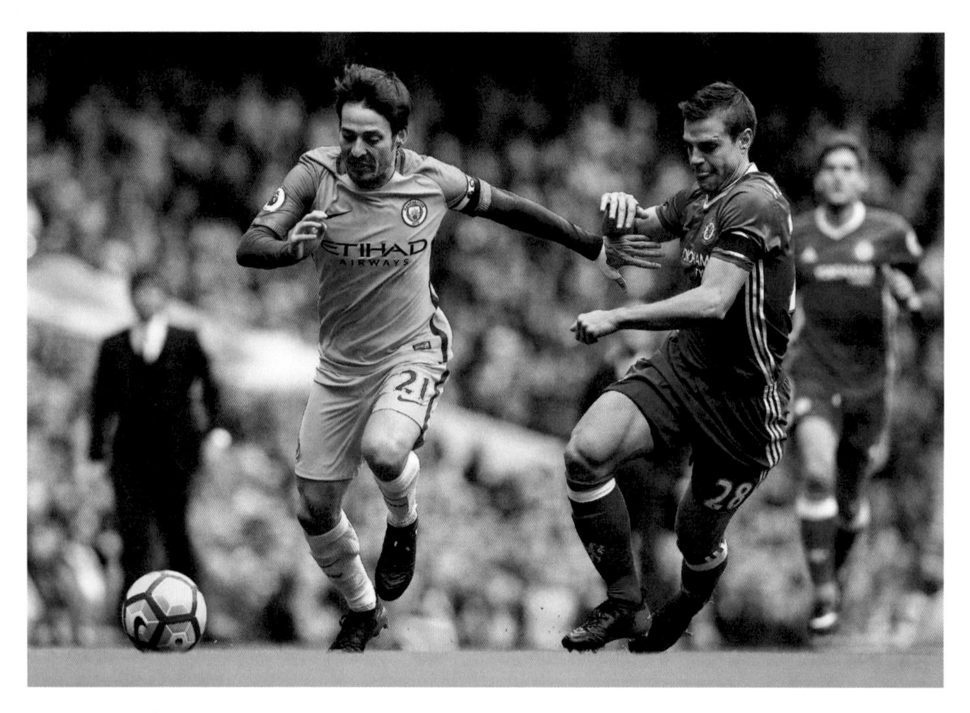

David Silva of Manchester City drives to the goal against Chelsea.

RONDO EXERCISES AND POSITIVE TRANSITION

In recent years, Rondo exercises have been highly emphasized training tools for soccer coaches, used for everything from training the first and second defender roles to warm-ups and pressure technical training.

Rondo training is also a highly effective means of focusing on breaking pressure in positive transition. In other words, in the moment that the ball is won, if the opponent makes a concerted effort to win back the ball, the team will need to be able to keep the ball in tight space and under extreme pressure. Rondo training simulates that pressure and forces players out of their comfort zone with regard to speed of play and speed of thought. An effective Rondo exercise is conducted in tight space, forcing players to move and think at the speed they will need to play in tight space in transition and compelling them to sharpen their vision with regard to the best choices to make in possession. As mentioned above, the exercises also test the players' ability to cope with pressure on their technical receiving and passing as well.

Finally, the exercises chosen for inclusion here also show the variety and flexibility of Rondo training available.

Two-Ball Rondo: Defeat Pressure

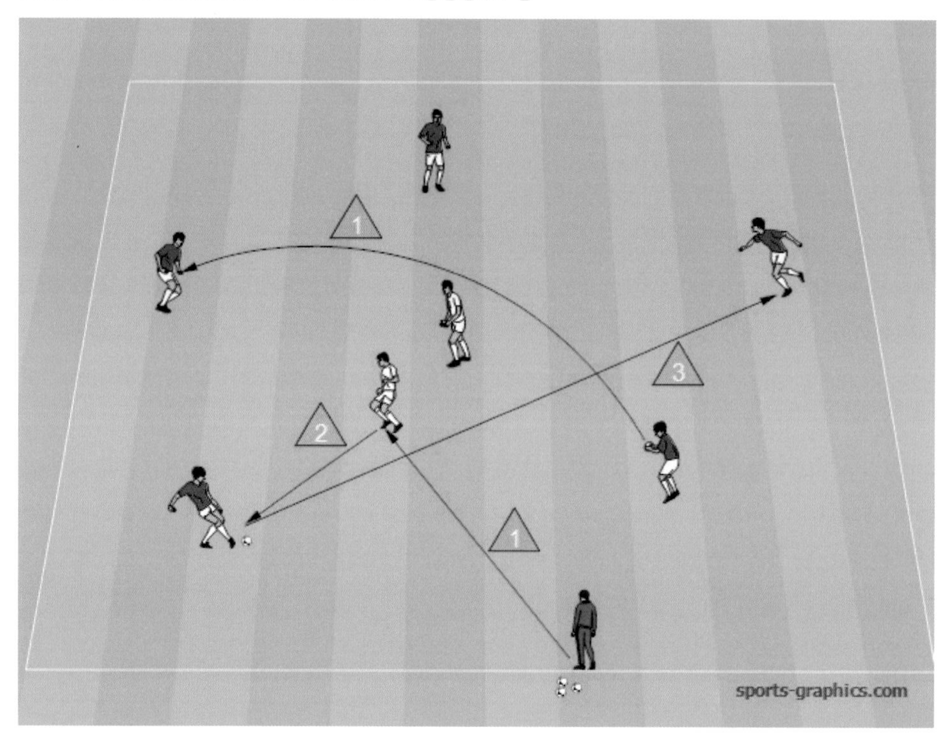

This is a standard 5 vs. 2 rondo in a 10 × 10 yard grid. Restarts commence with a pass from the coach to a defender, who turns the ball over to any attacker not holding a ball in his hands. The attackers then attempt to keep the ball for as long as possible. Meanwhile, the second ball in the grid is thrown and caught by the attackers at the same time. At no time may the player with the ball in his hands contact the ball being passed around at the attackers' feet. The defenders pay no attention to the ball being thrown by the attackers, but try to win the other ball and play to the feet of the coach. Rotate defenders after 1 minute.

COACHING POINTS

- Dealing with pressure and distraction. The attackers are essentially one person short in possession, as one man will have the thrown ball. That player must communicate and therefore distract another attacker. The attackers must learn to make good choices to keep both balls active.

- Movement. If all the attackers give their attention to one ball or the other, possession will break down. They must read the movements of the defenders and the other attackers and provide support to both soccer balls to continue to break pressure.

Bump Rondo: The Team Under Pressure in Possession With Movement

This is a great warm-up exercise for a session on offensive transition or a pressure possession exercise as the team learns to hold the ball in tight space in transition. Use four 10 × 10 yard grids. Two teams of eight, with two players for each team starting in the opposition grid as defenders, and another as an outlet target for the defending pair. The teams begin in opposite corner grids. The attacking players get one free pass with each restart and must connect six consecutive passes to move clockwise to the next grid. The movement to the next grid is live in the sense that the attackers must move there while keeping possession. When one team catches up to the other, its members holler "Bump!," and the other team does push-ups or crunches before the game is reset. When the defenders win the ball, they try to pass to their target outside the grid (target moves with the group). When the target receives, he steps on the ball, and the attackers have to retrieve it to restart. If the ball leaves the grid, the attackers get one free pass to restart play. Rotate the defenders after each bump.

COACHING POINTS

- Each restart or turnover retrieved by the attackers is an opportunity for the attackers to train on keeping the ball in tight space in transition.
- The technical quality of the players will be apparent in this environment. Loose touches, poorly weighted passes, and so forth, will cause breakdowns in the team's effort to keep possession.
- Movement within the area is critical. All four attackers without the ball must constantly adjust their positions to create *windows* through which the ball can be played to them. Sometimes this is a subtle movement, while other times players will have to move decisively to a new area of the grid.
- The player with the ball must have support options on either side and also a *split* pass available at all times.
- Require the attackers to count their passes out loud to practice communication under pressure.
- Help the players to understand that the movement to the next grid is part of their transition in possession. Connecting a few sharp passes often breaks an opponent's pressure and then the team can move into the next attacking space. Therefore, when the fifth pass is connected, the defenders do not quit, but rather they try to keep the ball in the grid. The attackers must move a target to the next grid and play the ball there before moving on as a group.
- By providing an outlet player for the defenders to pass to when they win the ball, another positive transition example is incorporated into the game.

VARIATIONS

- All restarts are throw-ins. If the ball leaves the area, the attackers throw it back in. If the defenders win the ball, they play their target, who throws the ball back to the attackers. In this way, playing in the air becomes a further technical demand.
- All passes to the next grid must be in the air. This requires some technical finesse in a tight space.
- If the defenders win the ball, they have to complete two passes before finding their target. The five attackers must win back the ball and keep it in transition.

Transitional Rhythm Rondo

Two teams of four players plus three neutral attacking players. The neutral players (yellow) remain in place throughout the exercise, though they should interchange positions with each restart to keep the center player fresh. The two teams of four (white, red) play against one another, with the team in possession (the white team here) being supported by the three neutral players. Note that the two teams of four change position with the loss of possession for the attackers. The change of position is live within the exercise, and the team shifting to defense should try to win the ball right away. Restarts come from the coach at the side of the grid, who passes in to a defender. The defender then passes to any attacker or neutral attacker to simulate a turnover.

COACHING POINTS

- On the turnover, can the attacking group develop rhythm passing to defeat the pressure of the defenders? The exercise provides both technical and oppositional pressure, as space and touch limits can be used to manipulate the environment to stress the attackers.
- Explain to players that this exercise is designed to focus on group dynamics when the ball is won. It is assumed here that no long pass and direct counter is available and that the attacking group will have to deal with the pressure of multiple defenders in tight space. The ball is very often lost in the few seconds after it is won. Can the group push through that critical time?
- Movement. Although the four attackers are on the sides of the grid, they must move for one another and their neutral attacker partners in possession. Passing angles must be created and recreated with every movement of the ball.
- Communication. Organizing around the ball when it is won can eliminate many turnovers. The environment should be lively, with the attackers calling for passes, and spreading ideas with each new pass.

VARIATIONS

- Touch limits. Give the attackers or the neutral attackers a two-touch or one-touch limitation to further pressurize the team in possession.
- Flying transition. When the defenders win the ball, the transition is live. In other words, the attackers must work to establish their shape, while the new defenders can try to win back the ball immediately. This restriction can create some chaos, even with advanced players, but it does replicate match situation transition.

- Add numbers. Adding a fifth attacker to each team (the fifth player is active in the grid with the defender and neutral attackers) further complicates the environment, and the added defender also builds the challenge.

Michael Bradley of the United States Men's National Team prepares to change the point of attack.

Sliding Rondo (4 vs. 2): Changing the Point in Transition

When the ball is won, the team must make a snap decision about how to keep the ball and go forward. This exercise helps players understand the potential need to relieve pressure with a few short sharp passes and then find an outlet that breaks pressing by opponents. Use two 12 × 12 yard grids separated by a 12 × 8 yard central space. The coach has a ball supply for restarts. Two defenders (white) receive the ball from the coach for the restart, and they immediately turn the ball over to the three attackers in the grid. Note that two additional attackers (red) are located on the extreme end of the grids. These players cannot enter the grid, and they do not move with play. Thus, the duel in the grid functions as a 4 vs. 2 possession exercise. The attackers try to keep the ball and when they have a window, they must try to play the attacking player (red) at the far end of the other grid. When that happens, the three attackers (blue) and the two defenders (white) sprint to the other grid and play continues. Note that the red players do not change grids at any time. If the defenders win the ball, they play to the coach and exchange roles with the attacker responsible for the loss of possession for the attackers (rotate).

COACHING POINTS

- Mobility in transition. When the ball is won, how long does it take players to recognize and play the far target? This ball is critical to releasing pressure and facilitating counterattacking and must be played as soon as a window is available.
- How should the attackers play in possession, knowing they need an outlet?

  1. The players need to try to array themselves in the grid to create an open window to the outlet. In other words, they need to try to avoid facing away from their attacking goal, and to be side-on, able to face up very quickly and deliver the longer pass.
  2. Mobility matters. In the grid, if play is stagnant and defenders win some of the balls off the attackers, explain that with 4 vs. 2, the attackers should be able to keep the ball and find the outlet within a few passes. Movement in the grid will make it harder for the defenders to isolate and win the ball.
  3. Communicate. The attackers know where the ball must go. They need to speak up, just as they should in the real match, and encourage the person in possession to quickly play the target when an angle is available.

VARIATIONS

- Serves into the grid from the coach are made in the air. Many turnovers happen in the air and the ability to settle and keep the ball while looking to change the point is very important.
- The extra attacker in each grid (red) is limited to one-touch play. This restriction adds pressure to the attacking group by limiting the involvement of the extra attacker.
- The pass to change grids from the attackers must travel *over* the center zone in the air. One again, this is a technical challenge to deliver a quality pass in the air, and it pressurizes the attackers as they look to change the point.

Transitional Rondo: 3 vs. 3 plus 3

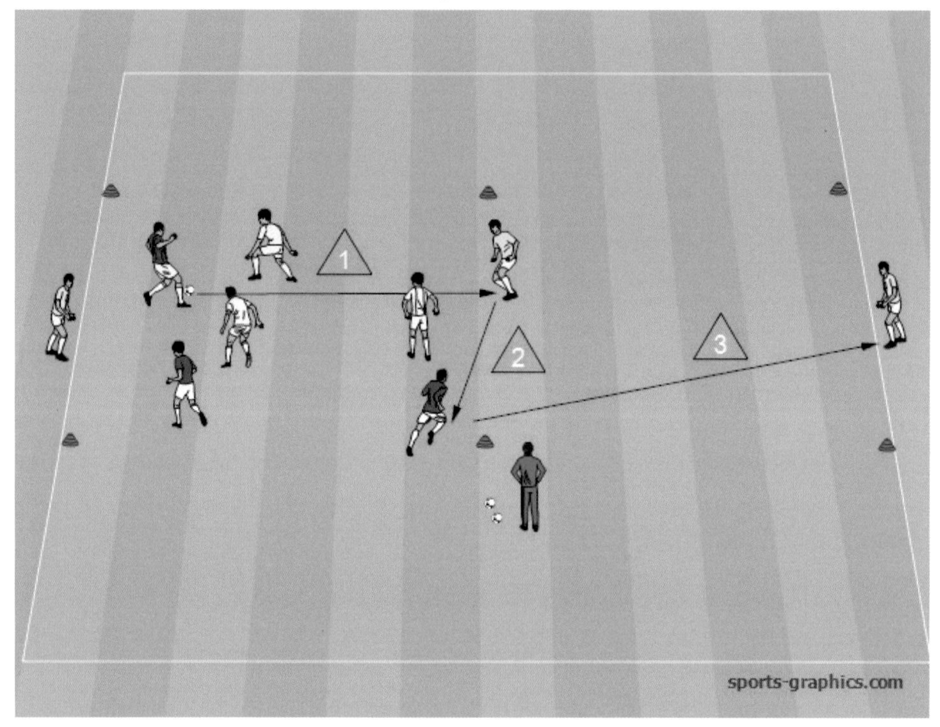

This environment challenges players to win and keep the ball in tight space, as well as finding an outlet and running off the ball in transition. Play 3 vs. 3 in one grid (red vs. white) in two 12 × 12 grids as shown. The neutral players play with the team in possession. The reds try to play into the feet of the yellow player in the center of the area. This player cannot enter the current 3 vs. 3 grid (i.e., the left side above) and must play one touch to a member of the attacking team as shown. That player can then play into the yellow target at the far end of the playing area. Note that the yellow players on the ends are confined to the end lines and cannot enter play at any time. Completing the outlet pass to the far end of the grid earns a point for the team in possession. If the defenders win the ball, they must play off the yellow or neutral player at the end line and then try to find the yellow player at the center of the grids to play out.

COACHING POINTS

- The movement and preparation of the attacking team under pressure. The group is working to relieve pressure and also try to get one of its members faced up with the center neutral to find the outlet pass.
- Early running in support of the pass to the center neutral. In the example above, the red player has recognized that his support of the ball in transition will give him an open look at the far target.

Triangle Midfield Rondo: Functional Horizontal Change in the Point of Attack (1)

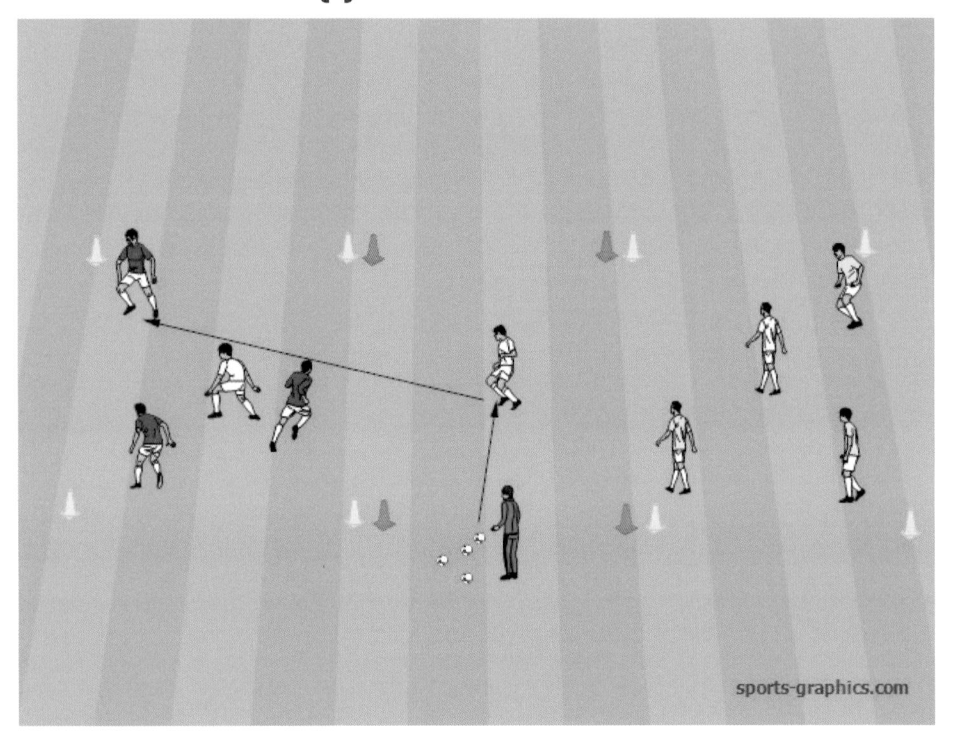

This has three teams of three players in three small grids. The defending team (white above) places one player in each grid. Those players must remain in their grids. The coach restarts play from the perimeter of the grids with a pass to the central defender, who passes to any attacker in either end grid (simulating a turnover). The attacking team must transition through the two grids to the opposite side of the playing area, all the while keeping possession. When they arrive in the far grid, they keep possession and play to the other attacking trio, who move to the far grid (where the sequence started) when the first trio arrives (see diagram 2 below). This delay compels the attackers to keep possession under pressure until an outlet pass can be identified. Note that the defenders are live whenever the ball is in their area. When the defenders win the ball, they pass immediately to the coach and play is restarted (simulating further transitional movements between defending and attacking). Rotate the defending group frequently to assure pressure is applied to the attacking groups.

Arguably the best midfielders of a generation: Andres Iniesta (left) and Sergio Busquets (right) of FC Barcelona and Andrea Pirlo (center) of Juventus

Triangle Midfield Rondo: Functional Horizontal Change in the Point of Attack (2)

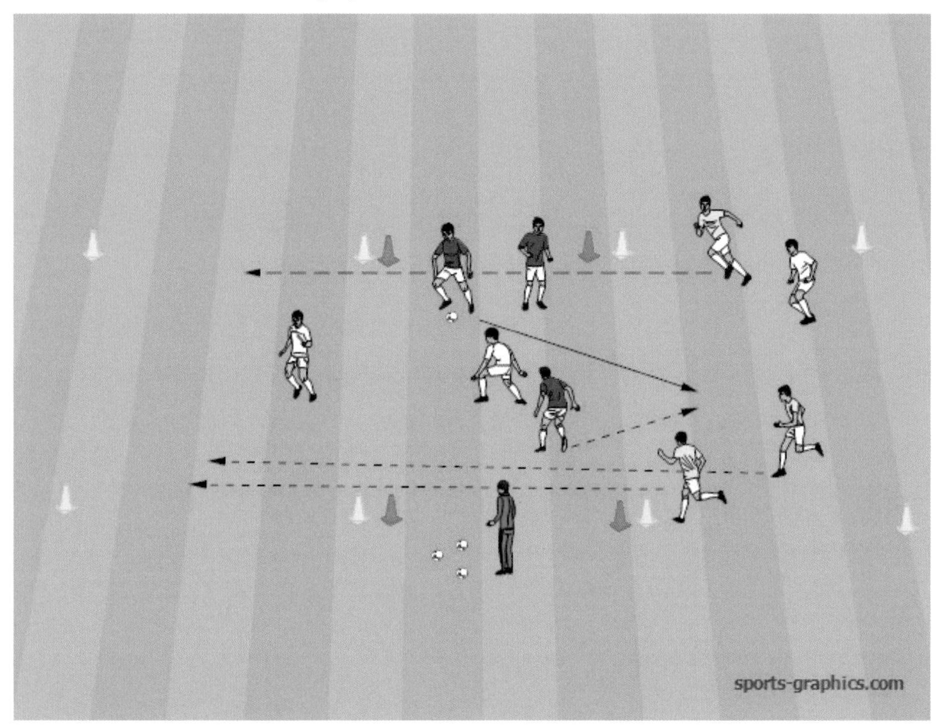

COACHING POINTS

- Explain that this exercise is functional in nature for players who operate out of a triangle midfield. Look for the attackers to consistently stretch and adjust their triangle, keeping good passing lanes and looking for opportunities to push on to the next area.

- Recognize the earliest opportunities to move. Three versus one in each grid should allow the attackers to establish possession quickly and look to move into the next area. A crucial learning moment is for the players to collectively recognize the need to move on to the next grid while being safe in possession. Central midfielders must always balance this risk/reward equation, seeking to open play into space while also supporting the ball against pressure.

- The quality of the outlet pass is essential. Once the trio have beaten the two defenders in the first two grids and become established in the third grid, they must find the moment to play into the far grid. This opportunity closely replicates the moment of a break in the real game, as the attackers are faced with three defenders trying to intercept their pass over distance. Coach the receiving targets to be active, checking in and out and evading the lone marker in their grid, and the team in possession to be patient as well as decisive in selecting and delivering a crisp outlet to the target.

VARIATIONS

- Touch limits for the attackers to apply further pressure.
- A minimum or maximum number or type (e.g., off foot only) of passes in each grid for the attackers.
- The long pass to a target must be made in the air. This restriction adds further technical demands to both the player passing and the player receiving.

4 vs. 4 plus 2: One-Touch Possession in Transition to Break Pressure

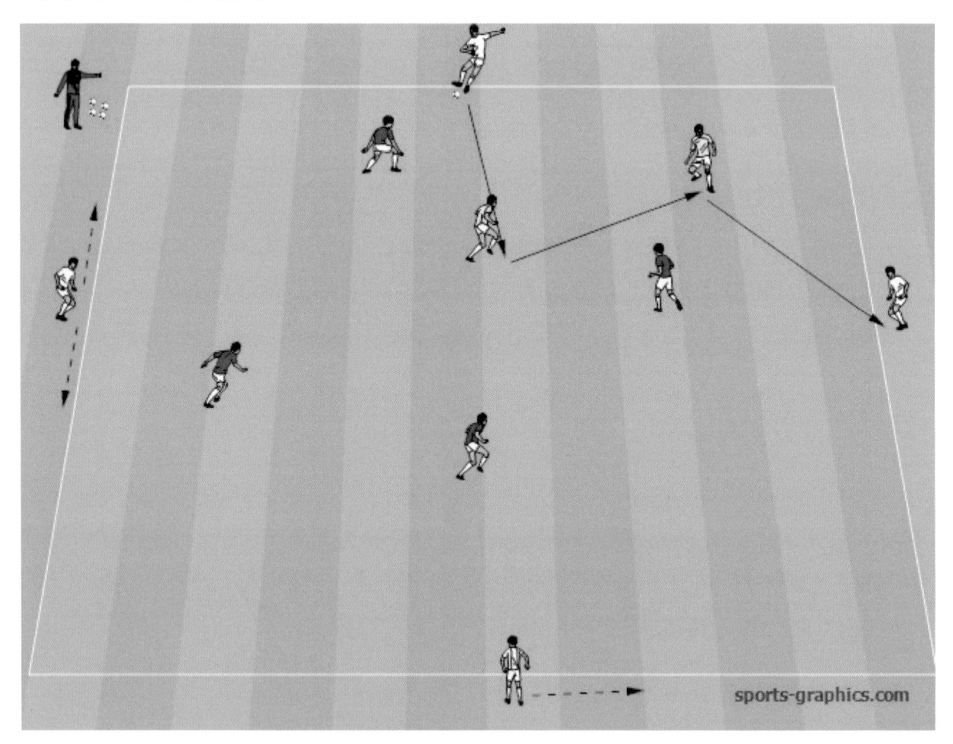

Play 4 vs. 4 plus 2 neutral players for possession. The team in possession works to get to the perimeter of the grid, with one player on each side. They use the two neutral players to help them keep possession. The four defenders are free to move inside the grid, trying to win the ball. It is useful, for the sake of developing rhythm, to play without touch restrictions in transition to start. In other words, when the defenders win the ball, they have unlimited touches to try to get established around the perimeter. Once they step over the perimeter, they are on one touch. For advanced players, once the exercise is running smoothly, the one-touch restriction can be instituted throughout (allow a player winning the ball two quick touches).

COACHING POINTS

- This is a true transition exercise in the sense that when the ball is won, the team will experience immense pressure from converging opponents while they try to expand their shape and poise to counterattack. It is important that players recognize that while this is not a functional exercise in the sense of playing in game-day positions, the environment replicates well very critical moments in the game.

- Thinking ahead. When the ball is won, or about to be won, what should each player do? Move closer in support or get to the perimeter and get established as an outlet target? Every situation will be different, and players must work together to solve pressure and keep the ball.

VARIATION

- Neutral players cannot play each other. This restriction forces the active players on the perimeter to move more and play longer to keep possession, both useful characteristics in many counterattack situations.

4 vs. 3 (8 vs. 6) Transition

This is an outstanding environment for creating rapid and frequent transitions. Two teams of eight and six play for possession. The attacking team is divided into two groups of four, each isolated in the first phase on opposite ends of the grid. The team of six is also divided into two groups and located in the center strip between the two grids. The coach initiates each sequence with a pass into one end of the grid. When the ball enters the grid, three defenders from the center strip also enter and try to win the ball. The attackers try to string together six passes. When they get to six, they earn a point and can try to play the ball to the other half of their team at the far end of the grid. If that happens, the three defenders return to the center strip, and their teammates enter the other half of the grid to try to win the ball. If the defenders win the ball, they try to keep it, and the center strip becomes null and void while the defenders have the ball. In other words, play 8 vs. 6 throughout the grid until the defenders lose the ball. If the defenders manage six passes, they earn a point. If the ball leaves the grid, players return to their respective start zones, and the coach restarts with a pass to one attacking group.

COACHING POINTS

- The exercise can be tweaked to emphasize many aspects of transition, from hunting the ball on defense to expanding the shape in possession and quick shifts back and forth with necessary surges of collective energy to either win or keep the ball.
- For the current context of having just won the ball, both teams can work on trying to get good support to the ball and rapid ball movement to break pressure. The outlet pass (to the other grid) is also an important consideration.
- For the defending team, when the ball is won, what is the team's shape? Can the group assess and reshape well enough to keep the ball for a few passes when outnumbered?

FOCUS ON SKILL: LONG PASSING

The ability to change the point of attack through long passing is essential to efficient counterattacking. Whether it's a long ball from an outside back to the back charging forward on the opposite side of the field or a cross served in by a forward, every player on the field needs to be able to serve the ball over distance with both feet. Additionally, the ability to choose and deliver the *correct* type of pass is critical.

There are three kinds of long passes:

1. Lofted. This service travels over distance and most often over players as well. The lofted pass is struck with pace by using the laces and striking the ball below center, causing great lift. This pass can be used to change the point of attack anywhere on the field.

2. Driven. The driven pass is used to move the ball to another part of the field, over distance, as quickly as possible. Height is not critical, and the ball is struck with the laces along the back (similar to shooting at pace). This pass has the advantage of great speed but is generally less accurate.

3. Chipped. This is a specialized pass used to reach a specific target, often in behind or in a crowd, and to give that target the opportunity for easier control on reception. The pass is struck with the laces, well below center back, and by halting the follow-through at the moment of striking, the passer applies backspin to the ball. That spin helps the pass float and also reduces backspin and bounce.

In addition to these three types of pass, there are other important means of influencing the ball (for example bending) that players can learn to give them the ability to deliver a ball that can facilitate effective counterattacking.

Kevin de Bruyne of Manchester City strikes a driven cross against Borussia Monchengladbach.

Driving Range Pairs Long Passing

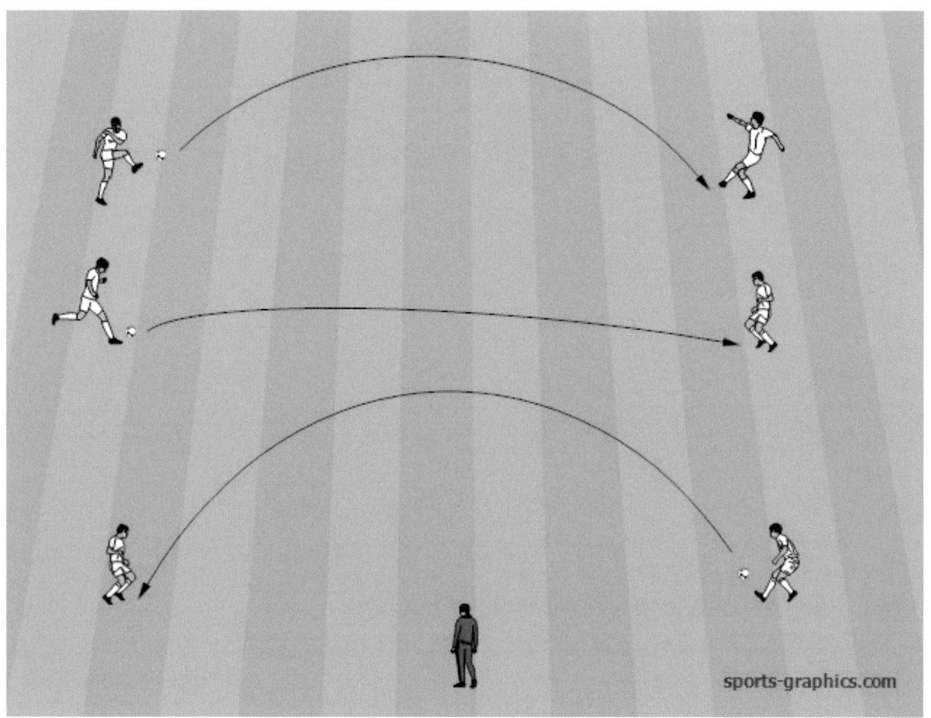

Players work in pairs over distance, practicing driven, lofted, and chipped passes, as well as receiving. This is a terrific means of allowing players a few minutes to train on their ability to play over distance and a great opportunity for the coach to help the players make technical corrections to their ball-striking. The coach can require a particular pass (or foot) to be worked on or allow the players time to experiment with spinning (bending) the ball or seeing who can strike the ball over the most distance. For younger players, placing a goal(s) down the middle of the area can be a useful visual aid for the players to practice striking lofted and chipped balls *over* the target.

Accuracy Long Passing 4s

Players work in pairs and play against another pair in a foursome. One member of each pair goes to each end of the playing area. Two cones are placed 30 yards apart (adjust according to the ability of the players to deliver the pass). Pairs alternate passing over the distance between cones. The goal is to receive the pass in the air and place it with one touch as close as possible to the cone. If the ball contacts the ground before the receiving player can touch it, the team loses that round. The team whose ball rolls to a stop closer to the cone earns a point. Players alternate roles as passer and receiver. The first team to score three points wins.

COACHING POINTS

- Quality lofted passes. Technique is isolated in this environment, with the opportunity to observe foot placement, striking, follow-through, and so forth.
- The importance of the receiving touch, which is paramount here. A first-rate receiving touch can clean up a poor serve, whereas a poor touch is punished, just as in the real game.
- Use of the nonpreferred foot to pass and receive.

Corner Targets Counterattacking

This is an outstanding environment for teaching players to recognize and coordinate counterattacking in a game setting. Though larger numbers will also work, the example above shows 6 vs. 6 functioning as 4 vs. 4 with two corner targets for each team. Restarts come from the coach at the side of the grid. Teams try to gain possession and then play in to one of their corner targets for a point. Teams must alternate the corner to that they play, and the player who passes in to the target takes that player's place and play continues.

COACHING POINTS

- The pass in to the target both symbolizes and replicates the opening outlet pass in a counterattacking move. The teams should be encouraged to play the pass in to the target as soon as possible. Sometimes there will be pressure and no clear path, and the team will need to be patient, but there will also be moments when the ball is won and the long pass will be *on*, and the team must move quickly to get the ball to the target.

- This exercise also lends itself to considerable repetition of counterattacking moves, as every ball in to a target restarts the sequence. Thus, the coach can imprint good attacking habits upon team members, including good supporting angles, combination play, changing the point of attack, team shape in the counterattack, communication, and so forth.
- Tempo is also a consideration. Counterattacking is about speed of recognition and thought, speed of movement, and speed of execution. This exercise facilitates training these elements.

VARIATIONS

- Limit the time or number of passes allowed to complete a pass to the target to encourage speed in the attack.
- The coach calls random turnovers. At a verbal signal from the coach, the team in possession must pass to the nearest opponent. This type of random turnover helps accelerate the team's ability to react to sudden opportunities in a match.
- Add a goalkeeper as a neutral player. The goalkeeper can play with his hands and may distribute to the target.

Playing good football is not related to style, but rather efficiency. –Carlo Ancelotti

FOCUS ON SKILL: TURNING

Among the necessary technical ingredients for effective counterattacking is turning. This skill is undertaught and underemphasized in the youth game, where "play the way you're facing" is a common credo. On the contrary, the willingness to turn, often under pressure, is often mandatory to the middle stages of a counterattack, when midfielders and forwards receive the ball and continue the momentum of the attack by trying to get faced up with the goal before dribbling or playing forward. Indeed the ability of the holding midfielder (the *pivot*) to turn (and know when to turn) in the professional game today is among the most important technical requirements for teams in possession and particularly for counterattacking. The series of exercises below present a number of ways to train the technical aspects of turning and also the important communication from nearby teammates that helps the player on the ball decide when and where to turn.

Sergio Aguero of Manchester City prepares to turn against Southampton.

Pairs Basic Turning (1)

Players work in pairs with one soccer ball. Utilize a grid 20 × 20 yards or longer, depending on the number of players. Place a line of cones down the center of the grid area. Players begin on the opposite side of the grid from their partner. The partner without the ball runs (checks) to the center of the grid. The partner with the ball passes on the ground to the checking player and then instructs him to "Turn!" The receiving player turns and dribbles back to his starting point. The players then change roles and play continues.

COACHING POINTS

- Communication. The player making the pass must instruct his partner to turn.
- Vision. The checking player must check his space (look over his shoulder to the space in which he intends to turn) while moving toward his partner.
- Turning technique. The receiving player should be side-on, which is to say he should point one shoulder toward the player passing the ball. In so doing, the player sets

himself up as half-turned before he receives. The receiving player should also make his first touch with the foot farthest from the server, allowing the ball to travel across his body. This facilitates the fastest, most efficient turn.

- Speed after the turn. To exploit the space and time allotted him by the pass, the receiving player should get in the habit of running and dribbling at speed back to his starting point.

Pairs Basic Turning (2)

In this variation, the receiving player is told "Man on!" from the server. He therefore gets side-on and receives with the outside of the foot closest to the passer. This body posture and receiving touch put him into a shielding position, where he can keep his body between the ball and the defender (the coach can add shadowing defenders if desired). On safely receiving, the player touches back toward the server and passes back before running back to his starting point. Note the addition of waiting soccer balls on the opposite side of the grid. Players change roles.

COACHING POINTS

- Communication. The "Man on!" call from the server is important to helping the receiving player understand his tactical options.
- Vision. The checking player should continue to check over his shoulder to fill in his vision.
- Receiving technique. The first touch with the outside of the away foot should be short enough to establish control without getting the ball stuck underneath the receiving player. The pass back should be sharp, and the player should then get out of the space as quickly as possible.
- Practice receiving with both feet.

Pairs Basic Turning (3)

Self-pass. The server calls "Man on!," and the receiving player decides to keep the ball and face up the defender. Note in the example above that the receiving player still receives with the outside of his away foot (from the defender). He then touches the ball back into negative space (usually 1–2 yards) and runs around the ball before dribbling back to his start point. Players then change roles.

COACHING POINTS

- Communication. The "Man on!" call is still part of the receiving player's vision.
- Vision. Continue to check the turning space while checking to receive.
- Turning technique. It is useful to add shadow defenders for this particular variation. If the defender is tight to the receiving player, the latter should *carve* into the defender (i.e., step into him) while the ball is traveling to him. This action will halt the defender's progress and allow the attacker to get separation after the first touch.
- The quality of the first touch, which must allow separation and time for the attacker to run around the ball and face up.
- Footwork. How quickly can the player run around the ball? Is he balanced?

1 vs.1: Getting Turned

The attacking player starts the sequence back to back with the defender, as shown in the diagram. He then checks away and returns, creating space. The waiting player at the bottom of the grid passes in to the feet (or space, depending on the indication of the target player) of the attacking player, who tries to turn and dribble out the defending player's end of the grid. If the defender can win the ball, he tries to dribble out the attacker's end of the grid. When the ball leaves the grid, the players change ends, and the next duel is initiated.

COACHING POINTS

- The importance of checking away to create space to turn.
- The use of the arms and the rest of the body to control and predict the movements of the defender.
- Communication (verbal, physical) to set the timing and location of the pass.
- The use of different types of turn.
- Playing at speed.

Transition Possession Game: Line Targets

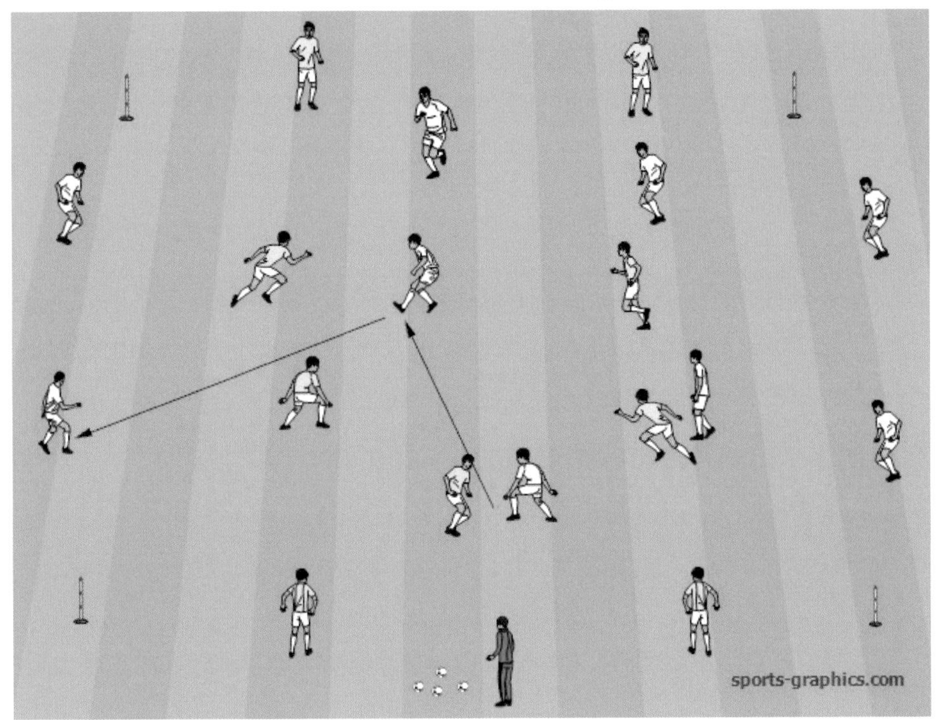

Play 5 vs. 5 plus four perimeter targets (two on opposing lines for each team). Restarts come from the coach at the side of the grid and can be played to either team. Teams attempt to play in to their targets as early and often as possible. It is mandatory that they alternate the side-on that they score (they must alternate the side to that they play). The target receiving the pass dribbles on and joins play, while the player passing into the target takes the target's place on the perimeter.

COACHING POINTS

- Recognize the moment to play the target. This is a busy environment and young players in particular often get wrapped up in the next pass and do not see windows to the two targets, who should be played as soon as possible to release pressure and find the outlet.
- Encourage players to think of each score here as a turnover situation, which is to say that a new attack starts as the target player receives the ball and joins play. In this way, the training takes on a more practical mind-set.

- Given the emphasis on turning in the previous section, take a moment to talk with players about the technical aspects of turning in this environment. Because of the many changes in the direction of play, there will be many opportunities to turn under pressure. Once again, knowing when to turn and helping one's teammates know when to turn and when to protect the ball is also an important, coachable aspect of the game.

VARIATION

- All passes in to target players must be made in the air. This adds technical demands on the passer and also the target, who must receive and get the ball settled before opposition pressure arrives.

Mobility in Attack: Four-Goal Soccer

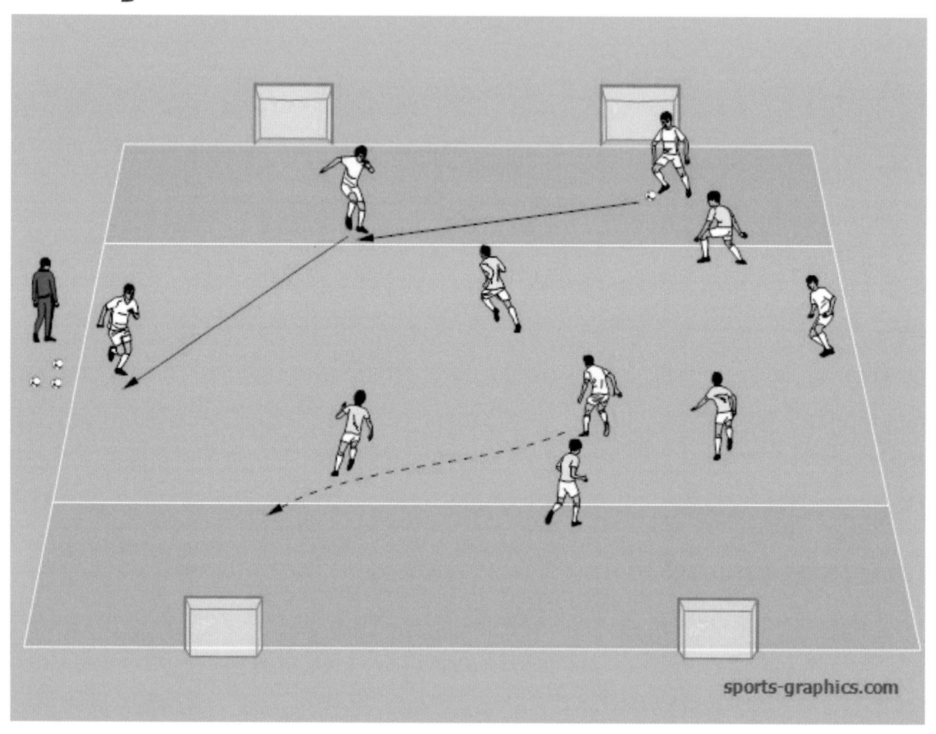

Two teams of five or more players play to four goals. Each team defends one end line and two goals. This is a popular possession game that compels players to recognize that an attack is not on when the defense concentrates near one goal and the attack must be quickly redirected to the other goal to gain an advantage. In the example above, the white team is in good attacking shape and appears poised to attack the yellow team's right-side goal. However, the yellow team's defense is heavily imbalanced to stymy just such an attack, and the white team opts to change the point of the attack quickly and attack the other goal. Restarts come from the coach and when a pass is received from the coach, the ball must be turned over to the other team (simulating a counterattacking opportunity).

COACHING POINTS

- Read the game through the defense. Almost invariably in this game one goal is easier to attack than the other, and the situation constantly evolves to create new opportunities on one side or the other.

- Change the point to unbalance the defense. Challenge the players to play *forward* and change the point.

- Team shape. One of the most difficult aspects of coaching counterattacking is the fact that every attack looks a bit different, starts from a different position, involves different players, and so forth, so it is difficult to rehearse set patterns beyond the basic principles. However, getting the shape right allows the team to expand the attack horizontally and vertically and challenge the defense with some predictability and coordination. In the example above, the fact that the wide player away from the ball has stayed near the edge of the grid has allowed his team to change the point and unbalance the defense without a lot of physical movement, meaning the move can be executed rapidly.

- Speed. To emphasize speed in the attack, limit the number of passes or time in possession for each team before a goal is scored. In this instance, this is not a probing environment, but rather an opportunity to work on quickly finding an opening and exploiting the defense.

VARIATIONS

- Pass limit and/or time limit to score. Exceeding the limit results in an immediate turnover.
- Use the horizontal zones in the diagram to specify what teams need to do in transition, for example, only vertical passes from the team's defensive zone or a mandatory combination in the middle zone as part of any counterattack.

Direct Play in a Small-Sided Game: 4 vs. 4 plus Goalkeepers to Goal

Play 4 vs. 4 plus goalkeepers on a very narrow, long field. All restarts come from the coach, who passes in to one team for that team to turn over to its opponents with its first touch. The long, narrow field will compel teams to play forward quickly, simulating the style of play for a fast counterattack.

COACHING POINTS

- The four-player shape is ideal for the environment, allowing for a single defender, two midfielders, and a target player. The diamond shape is excellent for imprinting responsibilities and patterns. For example, the single target player must learn to post up on the lone defender and often will need to hold the ball in transition. Similarly, the two midfield players have space forward to run into, encouraging them to explore going forward with the ball.
- Tempo. This game should only last a few minutes but must be played at pace for the environment to simulate counterattacking transition moments in the real game.

VARIATIONS

- Add a horizontal cone line dividing the field in half. The attacking players from each team must remain in their team's front half. This rule will help the target remain in a good position to look for outlet passes.
- Limitations on the number of passes or time in possession to compel the teams to play quickly.
- No pass back to the goalkeeper. This rule will further force teams to play forward and fast.

The Speed Zone: Playing Fast Through the Middle Third

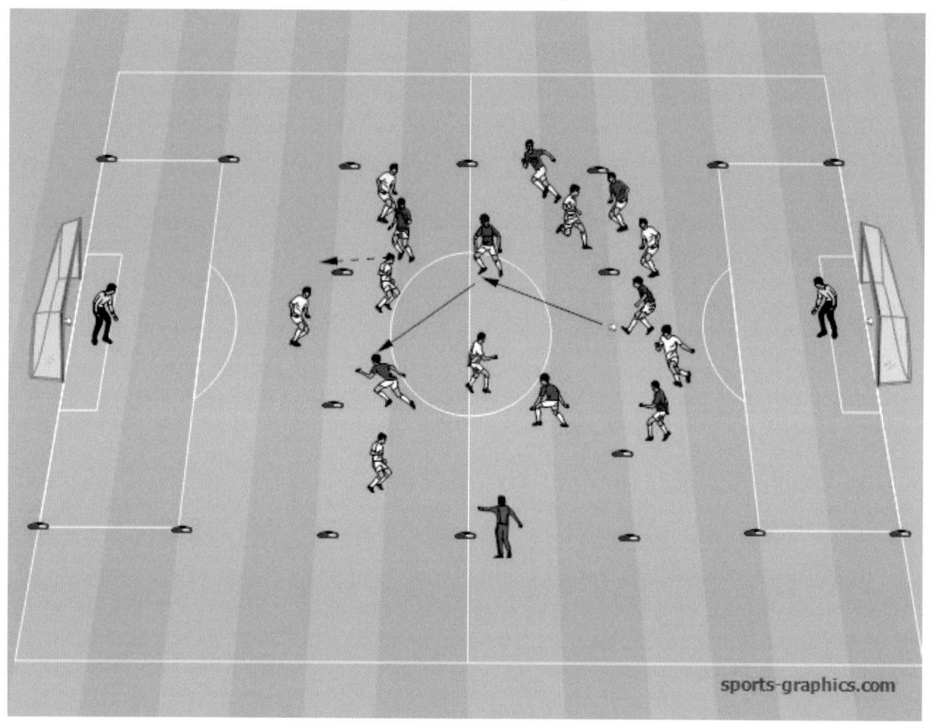

Play 8 vs. 8 plus goalkeepers on a full-sized field with the width cut to the sides of the 18-yard box and the field cut into thirds with cones. This is a standard match with restrictions placed on play in the middle one-third. Successful counterattacking often demands hard running and good, split-second decision-making through the middle third of the field. To emphasize speed in this zone, allow a limited number of passes (i.e., 3), touches (i.e., 6), or time (6 seconds) to play through this area. Any violation of the rule results in an immediate turnover.

COACHING POINTS

- Recognition of positive transition. When the ball is won, can the team get into attacking shape faster than its opponents can adapt to negative transition? Expanding team shape through early running will increase the likelihood of successful attacking.

- Decision-making on the ball. Can the player on the ball consistently select the proper pass? The proper pass in most cases is the safest, longest pass forward if the team wants to counterattack. Measuring risk is an acquired skill in transition.
- Communication. The team must work together to generate the counterattack in transition. An important component of the transition is communication. Getting players turned as they receive will speed transition, and communicating the correct pass will help build momentum in the attack. Conversely, failure to communicate means that the team is working with one mind at a time rather than a collective intelligence, and the chance of failure increases in isolation.
- Changing the point of attack. Often, a change in the point of attack will be required in the midfield, as the opponents' shape is distorted when they lose the ball. Can the team change its point of attack without losing momentum? The pass/touch/time limits will compel the team to think in terms of speed through the middle third, inclusive of needs to change the point of attack.
- Preferred runs. Training some specific patterns will help team cohesion in the transition process. For instance, if the team can rehearse runs by the strikers, both underneath to receive, and also penetrating, the team will attack more successfully. Similarly, the shape and running of the midfielders and the outside backs during positive transition should also be choreographed to the extent possible. Familiarity among the players in transition as to their teammates' movements will make it easier to maintain possession and move forward in unison.
- Mentality. Finally, the coach must also coach the mental state of the players in transition as well. Working through the middle third with speed requires determination, particularly as players tire during the match. The priority must be to wear down an opponent with speed and mobility, as well as endurance, and part of the demands placed on players in these circumstances is the need for mental toughness.

VARIATION

- Limit the movement of certain players on defense to facilitate more room for positive transition in the speed zone. For instance, if the forwards from a defending team cannot leave the front zone, two fewer defenders will be available to that team in negative transition. Similarly, if the team's defenders (or one or two defenders) cannot push forward into the speed zone, the middle zone will be more open, and the opponent will be able to push through the zone more quickly, highlighting the points of emphasis in the game.

Four-Zone Possession: Find the Outlet Pass With Pressure

Create two teams of 6-8 players, placing half of each team in alternating zones as shown above. The playing area will vary with the age and ability of the players, but each zone is typically 10 yards deep and 20–25 yards wide. The coach restarts play from the side of the grid as shown, passing in to any of the four grids. As shown above, the team in possession attempts to pass to its members in the other grid area, thus connecting an outlet pass simulating the commencement or continuation of a counterattack. The defending team can send two players into the grid once the ball is in the area. If the defenders win the ball, they attempt to dribble or pass the ball back to one of their own grids, and play continues. Note that if the ball is in one of the central grids, the defending team must send one player from *each* of its grids to defend (see the following figure).

Four-zone possession: defending a central grid. The emphasis here is on the attacking, but the slide is included to highlight how the game is played.

COACHING POINTS

- The importance of technique is highlighted in this exercise, as poor touches will result in more pressure and turnovers. Receiving touches, location, and weight of passes are all subject to scrutiny in this playing environment.

- Recognize the moment to play. At times, an immediate outlet pass is available, and the player may even want to pass first time to the other grid. If the defenders get in and apply pressure, the group will need to break that pressure with rapid ball movement to create an opportunity to play the outlet.
- Targeting. The players in the target grid must be constantly moving and looking for windows through which they can be played.

VARIATION

- Require all passes between zones be made in the air. This restriction places technical demands on the team in possession as it must be able to execute a chipped or lofted ball through occupied space to a target, and the target must be able to control the ball with pressure arriving.

Possession Game to Target Player in Central Zone

This exercise has the benefit of placing the target player in a central zone, similar to the location where many outlet passes must go in the full game. The teams play 5 vs. 5 plus a target player confined to the attacking zone. Restarts come from the coach at the side of the grid. All restarts are turned over immediately on receiving from the coach. Teams score points by successfully delivering the ball to their target players in the zone. The target player cannot leave the grid at any time. No defenders may enter the grid, nor can any member of the attacker's team enter the grid. When the target player receives the ball, he plays to the nearest member of the opposing team (turnover) and play continues, with immediate transition.

COACHING POINTS

- How early can the ball be played to the target player? If a long pass can be played into the target zone, the teams should try to reach the striker as soon as possible.
- Coach the use of angles to find the outlet/entry pass. The first effort will usually be from the central area (most direct), but it may be necessary to swing the ball out wide to find an angle of entry to the target, or perhaps the team will need to change the point of attack on multiple occasions to create the right angle of entry. Remember, however, that speed is critical (see variations to force more direct, urgent play).

VARIATIONS

- Limit the time a team has to play into the target to force the players to look to play fast.
- Limit the number of passes that the teams have to play into the target to compel the teams to play more quickly.
- When the target receives the ball, he tries to hold it for 3 seconds (opponents can enter the target grid to try to win the ball as soon as the ball enters the area). If he can, he is allowed to play back to his own team to restart play. This variation encourages the target to work on his hold-up play.

Mesut Ozil of Arsenal leads the counterattack against Paris-St. Germain in UEFA Champions League play.

Cobra Strike: Getting Forward in the Attack (1)

Play 3 vs. 3 or 4 vs. 4 to small goals in a grid that is divided in half with cones. The attacking player (target) for each team can only operate in the team's attacking half. The two defenders start in their defensive zone. They may not shoot at goal. They try to keep possession and then play in to their target when the pass is available. The player passing in to the target then joins the attack and can stay in the front half of the grid until the ball is lost or a goal is scored.

COACHING POINTS

- The movement of the attacker. The target has a tendency to sit near the center line and wait on a pass. Such habits make him easy to mark in this game and also in the full-sided game. Instead, he should be active, attempting to get out of the vision of one or both of the backs. It's important that the target understand that this sometimes means running into an offside position to create space and keep the backs from playing near the center line. The target must learn to read the play and body language of his supporting players to decide when to check in to receive the ball.

- Supporting runs. What is the best angle of approach and distance for players coming forward in support of the attack? These runners need to react to the body position of the target and the pressure being applied by the defenders. If the target gets turned, the supporting runner can make a penetrating run. If he is pushed into a shielding position, the supporting runner must get to an angle underneath where he can receive a supporting pass and then the two players must work together to break down the two defenders.

VARIATION

- When the ball is played to the target, the *other* player in the back half of the field must go forward to support the target (see diagram above). This requirement compels players to think in terms of running off the ball (i.e., third man running).

Connect With the Target Player

Groups of three players knock a ball in flank grids as shown above. At a signal from the coach, the player in possession passes in to the target player as shown. The players from the passing grid join the target player, and the group attacks the goal. When play is reset, the other grid makes the forward pass and follows on the counterattack.

COACHING POINTS

- The movement and communication of the striker. Working against dummies at this stage, he should learn to make useful, well-timed runs to find space and safely receive.
- The supporting runs. One runner should get under the ball immediately so that when the striker is confronted by real pressure in the game, he can lay off the ball and keep the momentum of the attack. Another runner should get up the flank on the near side, where there will likely be space when the ball is played into the target.
- Speed and creativity in the attack.

VARIATIONS

- Add recovering defenders who come out of the possession grids with the players who play into the target. These players are live throughout the counterattack unless they win the ball.

- Require a particular element in each counterattack.

  Examples
  1. Pass into the target must arrive in the air (to train on passing accuracy and the ability of the target to receive out of the air.
  2. A supporting pass underneath the target after he receives.
  3. A set number of changes in the point of the attack (recommend 2-3).
  4. Limit the time available for each attack or the number of passes.

Small-Sided Positive Transition from the Middle Third: 3 plus 1 vs. 2 plus 1 to Goal (1)

Play 3 vs. 2 in two grids near midfield as shown. One grid plays while the other rests and recovers. The focus is on the two defenders. When they win the ball, they must play to their teammate in open space at the entry to the front third. The player passing to the target then joins the attack and play 2 vs. 1 to goal (see diagram 2).

Small-Sided Positive Transition from the Middle Third: 3 plus 1 vs. 2 plus 1 to Goal (2)

When the action from the first grid has ended, a coach serves a ball into the second grid and play continues. Note that the colors/numbers are reversed in the second grid and that the roles of the two players awaiting the pass outside the grid are also reversed (see diagram 3).

Small-Sided Positive Transition From the Middle Third: 3 plus 1 vs. 2 plus 1 to Goal (3)

PROGRESSION

- When one player passes to the target, the other member of his team in the grid must join the attack.
- Add a recovering defender (see diagram 4) to the play. One of the group of three in the grid must track back and try to help break up the counterattack. This progression adds time pressure to the counterattackers, which can also be done through limits on time or numbers of passes.

Small-Sided Positive Transition from the Middle Third: 3 plus 1 vs. 2 plus 1 to Goal (4), With Recovering Defender

Getting Between the Lines: Transition Zone (1)–Striker Checking

Play 5 vs. 5 plus goalkeepers on one-half of the field, with the width trimmed to that of the 18-yard box. Each team plays 1-2-3-1. In the opening stage, simply play without restrictions. After the game has been played for a few minutes, introduce a narrow grid in the middle of the field. Explain that only the target player from either team can touch the ball in that area in transition. Other players can run through the zone but cannot play the ball while in the zone. Show how the team can use this space, which is between the opponents' back line and their midfield line, to break out on the counter. Compel both teams to play to their targets in this space when the ball is won in the back half of the field before going forward with their attack.

COACHING POINTS

- The timing of the striker's run. If they arrive too early, they will be marked. If they are too late, the play breaks down. The attacker must anticipate the effort by his teammates to find him and arrive with the ball in the space.
- Once the ball has been played to break the opponent's midfield line, what patterns does the coach want to see imprinted? With a few simple cues, the coach can start to show how the team will transition forward on the counter.

Getting Between the Lines: Transition Zone (2)—Midfielder Penetrating Run

Once the team has grasped the possibilities of the striker coming underneath to get between the opponent's lines, stop the game and show that the midfielder(s) may also get into this zone to receive and play out their opponents. As play proceeds, allow any of the midfielders or the forward to show in this space, but allow only one attacking player to be in the zone at any time.

COACHING POINTS

- Once again, the conditions for the run must be understood and reinforced. Midfielders cannot run in behind the opponent's midfield line unless possession is not threatened (as the run means they will not be readily able to defend in the event of a turnover) and if they can find a window from which to receive from their teammates behind them.

Gonzalo Higuain of Juventus comes underneath the Cagliari back line to receive in a Serie A match.

TRAIN THE TARGET PLAYER—HOLD UP PLAY

Train the Target Player: Hold-Up Play (1)

This is the first in a progressive series of exercises designed specifically to train the target player(s) in receiving and holding up play. The reliability of the target player in this role is essential to many direct counterattacking moves.

The coach serves balls on the ground for the target player to corral and hold for 3 seconds (counted aloud by the coach). The target player then returns the ball to the server. Instruct the defenders to vary their pressure and tracking of the target player at the outset of the exercise.

COACHING POINTS

- The movement and posting up of the target player. A striker who comes to the bottom of the grid and awaits the pass is easy to mark. On the contrary, an intelligent striker will attempt to start in or near an offside position (instruct the defenders to start in the far half of the grid) and check sharply to receive the ball. Additionally, the striker will need to check at angles to confuse the defenders as to which one of them should be marking the attacker. A good way to remember this is to make opposing runs, which is to say that if the intention is to check underneath, then the target should first check sharply away (go away to come back). In this way, the defense is confused, and space opens up.
- Communication. The attacker should communicate physically and verbally his desire to receive the ball.
- Physicality. The target will most often receive under considerable physical pressure. He must learn to get shoulder-on to the serve and shield the ball with his first touch.

PROGRESSION

- Serves in the air.
- Allow the target player to make check runs out of the grid (defender may follow).

Abby Wambach of the United States: prolific goal scorer and also a gritty, determined target player whose hold-up play was exemplary

Train the Target Player: Hold Up Play (2)

Add a midfield player to the attacking. This player cannot enter the larger grid until the target player makes contact with the ball in the grid, compelling him to briefly hold the ball while support arrives. The pair then plays 2 vs. 2 to the flag goals against the two defenders. If the defenders win the ball, they play to the coach to reset the sequence.

Train the Target Player: Hold Up Play (3)

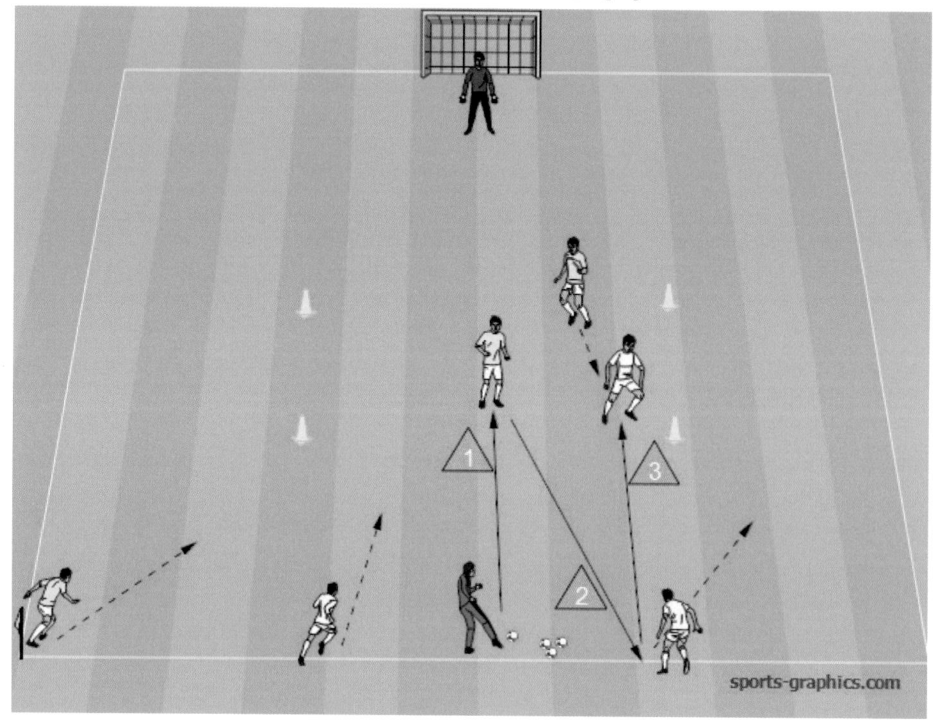

Here the exercise is expanded to encompass an entire attack. Add a recovering defender (lower left) and a goalkeeper defending the goal. Another supporting attacker also waits at the edge of the grid. The upshot is that play will evolve to 3 vs. 2 with a recovering defender to goal. The coach initiates the sequence with a pass to a defender in the grid. The defender turns over the ball with a pass to one of the midfielders, who passes in to the target. The recovering defender and the two supporting attackers join play as quickly as possible. If the defenders win the ball, they pass to the coach. The attackers try to score on goal, with speed being an important consideration.

VARIATIONS

- Allow the attackers a limited window to score (e.g., 10 seconds from the entry pass to the target).
- Add more players to create more complicated, functional, and realistic scenarios.

5 vs. 5 plus Targets Middle Third Transition

Play 5 vs. 5 (2-1-2 shape for each team) in the center grid. Each team places two targets in the end zone in front of its attacking goal. Restarts come from the coach at the side of the grid. At first, simply require a pass in to the striker's feet in the end zone to spring that player to turn and attack goal. Emphasize quality passing, looking to play forward and receiving side-on (half-turned).

VARIATIONS

- Require a particular sequence of passes in the buildup before the ball in to the striker (e.g., a 1-2).
- Require a ball in to the feet of one striker in the zone, a layoff and through-pass to release the other striker to goal.
- Require a more challenging pass in to the striker (e.g., ball served in the air).

7 vs. 7 plus Goalkeepers Zones Transition

Play 7 vs. 7 plus goalkeepers to full-sized goals on a normal or slightly shortened pitch that is as wide as the 18-yard boxes. The playing area is also divided horizontally in thirds as shown above. Play 5 vs. 5 in the center zone, and one player from each team is isolated in the front and back zones. This is a very flexible environment for training transition. In the basic phase of the game, the players in the end zones cannot leave those areas. Players from the central zone must play into their target and then two of them must join the attack once the ball enters their front third. One player from the center zone can also track back into the defensive third when the ball is played there (creates 3 vs. 2 to goal). When the attack ends, all players must return to their original zones. Restarts come from the coach at the side of the area.

COACHING POINTS

- Runs and behavior of target player. He must time his movements to show for the ball and be able to hold up play against the defender to allow an attack to develop.
- Getting players forward quickly after the ball is won. It will be necessary to sustain an attack (hoping for 3 vs. 1, or at worst 3 vs. 2).
- Speed and mobility in the attack. Because these should be numbers-up situations, driving the ball to the goal is mandatory. Running off the ball—early and to good angles to goal—needs to be consistent and creative.
- Recovery runs. When the attack breaks down, the team must recover quickly, as its opponents will gain a decisive advantage in the midfield if the defending team is without any of its players.

VARIATIONS

- Limit the number of passes or time allotted in possession to score to force teams to play forward.
- Require a particular type of pass into the target player (i.e., a pass into his feet or a serve from the backline player).
- Add players. Each team gets one more defender and another midfielder. When the ball is played to the target player, three attackers and one defender join from the middle third (creating 4 vs.3).

6 vs. 6 plus Goalkeepers to 6 vs. 3 Transition Game

This is a 6 vs. 6 plus goalkeepers scrimmage on half of the field. When one team scores, three members of that team must go finish a cross at the side goal while the team conceding the goal counterattacks the remaining three players from the team that tallied. Once they have finished a cross, the players rejoin their team in the run of play, and the game continues.

COACHING POINTS

- Transition. When a team scores, both teams have work to do immediately. Explain that this simulates a turnover situation, and one team gets to send members to finish a cross, while the other enjoys a temporary 6 vs. 3 advantage. Speed is of the essence for both teams.

- Principles of counterattacking. The team enjoying the 6 vs. 3 advantage should look for an immediate, long, safe outlet and look to goal with numbers and speed. If a long outlet is not available, the team must use sharp passing and combinations to break pressure and continue to change the point of the attack until a path to goal is available.

VARIATION

- The three players detailed to finish a cross cannot return until they score off a cross.
- Time or pass number limitations before a goal can be scored in the 6 vs. 6 format and for the team with the 6 vs. 3 advantage.

5 vs. 5 vs. 5 plus a Goalkeeper Transition Game (1)

Three teams of five compete on an area that is one-half of the length of the pitch and as wide as the penalty area. One team (red in the diagram) attacks the goal (attackers), while the white team defends (defenders). If the ball leaves the area, play is restarted by the goalkeeper, who plays out to the white team. The white team remains on defense until they can transition forward and make a successful pass to the blue team, who waits in the *transition* grid near midfield. If the red team scores, the goalkeeper distributes to the white team so that they can continue to try to transition forward. When the blue team receives the ball from the white team in the transition grid, they become the attacking team, working to goal, while red, who has failed to prevent the white team's transition, becomes the defending team. The white team jogs to the transition grid, and play continues.

COACHING POINTS

- The attacking team should attempt to score as quickly as possible after winning the ball. This exercise produces many opportunities for the attackers to cover the approaches to the goal by catching the defenders in a poor position. The other point of emphasis here is the need to press the defenders and not allow them to build or play out.

- The defending team needs to be encouraged to control the approaches to goal and then find the outlet pass to the transition grid as soon as an opportunity appears. Many players will get caught looking down and will fail to see the chance to push a ball to the outlet players on the third team in the grid. This is tantamount to failure regarding the chance to eliminate five opponents with a single pass on the counter.

- For the waiting team in the transition grid, the time should be used to organize and discuss tactics on the counter. Should they work combinations to break down the defenders, or should they try to just get in behind with a quick vertical ball when they get out of the grid? Much will depend on the shape of the defenders as possession is won in each instance, but communication and known tendencies will make for more efficient counterattacking.

5 vs. 5 vs. 5 plus a Goalkeeper Transition Game (2)

This figure shows the importance of quick transition in this exercise. The red team has attempted to play a long diagonal ball to put an attacker in on goal (1). However, the white defender has read the pass, and he steps up to cut out the long ball. He then recognizes that he is not under pressure as he receives, and he immediately plays to the blue team in the transition grid (2).

5 vs. 5 vs. 5 plus a Goalkeeper Transition Game (3)

Variation: This is the same as game 2, but with rule changes to further accentuate transitional moments. The waiting blue team now places three players in the transition grid and the remaining two players on either flank, as shown. The blue players outside the grid are not active until the blue team gains possession in the grid and begins their attack. When the ball is played into the grid by the defending (white) team, the red team can enter the grid and try to win back the ball before the blue team can get their attack started. The blue team must connect four passes before they can exit the grid toward goal. If the red team wins the ball in the grid, they can continue to attack. If the blue team connects four consecutive passes, the teams change roles, with white moving to the grid, red now defending, and blue attacking. As shown in the figure, the white team has built out and played into the blue team in the grid. Red players move quickly to try to disrupt the blue team's possession.

COACHING POINTS

- It's best to play the base game (described previously) first to help players acclimate to the environment. This game can be chaotic for younger players.
- This exercise presents interesting tactical challenges for all three teams throughout the game. The defenders are encouraged to win possession and successfully complete transition forward so that they can get out of the defending role. For the attacking group, they have incentive to defend when they lose the ball all the way up to the fourth pass in the transition grid, as they might win back the ball and be able to go on attacking. For the team in the transition grid, they must solidify their possession and break pressure with quick passes before springing forward. All these rolls highlight the various moments in transition and help players and groups understand the need for early action and sharpness as the game changes.
- Do the players recognize their roles in transition? Do the attackers recover to cut out passes to the transition grid, or do they let up and allow the defenders out? Do the attackers sprint into the transition grid to break up the possession of the team trying to get established there? Does the team in the transition grid use good spacing, limited touches, and movement to break up the attackers' pressure? Do the defenders, once their team has completed their buildout and transition, recover quickly to the grid (which simulates clearing lines in the real game)?

VARIATIONS

- Require the defenders to complete a certain number of passes or a combination in their buildout, or, limit their touches and passes if the goal is to get them to play in a more direct fashion out of the back.
- The attackers have a limited time or number of passes to score. This restriction can be used to get them to attack the goal more quickly, and also to ensure more transitional moments. If they fail to score in the set time or number of passes, they give the ball to the defenders (who must still build out), and play continues.

World Cup 2018: Argentina vs. Iceland at the Spartak Stadium, Moscow: Alfred Finnbogason scores as Iceland earns a 1-1 draw against one of the tournament favorites. Iceland's stout defending, along with their spirited counterattacking, frustrated the talented Argentinians.

6 vs. 6 vs. 6 Transition Game

Three teams of six play to full-sized goals with goalkeepers. One team attacks a second team (white attacks blue above) while the third team (yellow) rests. When red wins the ball (or white scores or plays the ball out of bounds), the red team will advance to try to score on the yellow team, while the white team rests. This is a continuous game.

VARIATIONS

- Limit the time or number of passes for the attacking team to compel teams to attack quickly.
- Require the entire team to get forward beyond a given point (i.e., the top of the 18-yard box) before a shot on goal can be taken. This restriction encourages the entire group to attack and gets numbers to goal to increase the chance of scoring.
- Require goals be scored from a certain buildup (i.e., cross).
- Require defending teams to come up to a given point at the start of an attack to create more play further from goal, and allow for a ball in behind the defending group.

Conditioned Game to Promote Counterattacking: 6 vs. 6 plus Goalkeepers

Play 6 vs. 6 on one half of the field to full-sized goals with goalkeepers. Use a cone line to split the field at the horizontal midpoint. The teams field three defenders, two midfielders and a target player. The target player is confined to the front half of the field for each team. When possession is gained, the team has 10 seconds (adjust the time allotted as needed) to score. Require teams to play through their target players in the breakout phase.

COACHING POINTS

- The movements of the target player. The forward is outnumbered (one attacker vs. three defenders) and unable to check back into his team's half of the field to receive, so he will need to be very active and time his runs well to get on the end of outlet passes. He will need to practice opposite movements, checking away to create space before showing underneath and also conversely coming underneath to draw in defenders and then sprinting in behind the exposed back line.

- The quality of the outlet pass. The back five players and the goalkeeper need to be in tune with the movements of the target player for transition to be consistent and effective.
- Speed. The time limitation means that there is no room for wide attacks or long back passes. The teams must press home their attacks through hard running, forward passing, and driving the goal.

VARIATION

- Rather than a time limitation, use a touch restriction or limit the number of passes a movement can entail. Though these are different rules, they still apply time pressure to the team in possession.

Situational Counterattacking: Counter After a Cross

This is a simple setup to encourage players to think about counterattacking even when they're defending in their back third. The white team provides servers on each flank who alternate dribbling to the end line and crossing. Inside the 18-yard box, there are three white attackers, three red defenders, and the goalkeeper. These players are all live when the ball is in the box. If the attackers score, they earn a point, and play continues with the next serve. If the defenders or the goalkeeper win the ball, they distribute the ball to the red targets, with preference for the red striker near midfield. The red players near midfield (3) then attack the two white defenders and try to score in the white goal (bottom). The white defenders must stay in the back half of the circle until the ball is touched by the red striker.

COACHING POINTS

- Transition play. How quickly can the red defenders find their outlet players and start the counterattack?
- Speed in transition. Limit the time the counterattacking red players have to finish their drive to goal.

VARIATIONS

- Add more counterattacking players (i.e., wings) and recovering white defenders.
- Make the white defenders live from the outset, and coach the runs of the red counterattackers.

Manuel Neuer of Bayern Munich and Germany starts the counterattack.

Situational Counterattacking: Counter vs. High Defensive Back Line

While often counterattacks are aided by strikers coming underneath to receive an outlet pass, some teams opt to deploy a high defensive line to hem in their opposition and make it very difficult to find space underneath the back line where a target can receive the ball. The solution to this dilemma is for the counterattacking team to play in behind the high back line. In the exercise above, teams play 2 vs. 2, knocking the ball around until a signal from the coach lets loose the team in possession. The attacking target player (white) recognizes the lack of space underneath and makes a check run away from the ball and the center backs (red) before timing his run in behind. Note that his run puts him on the back shoulder of the defender, where he is hard to track. The three players (two attackers and the target) then drive home their attack against the two defenders and the goalkeeper.

COACHING POINTS

- Coordinating the attack. It is critical that both the target and the midfielders, coming out of the grid, make the same read regarding the defense. If the attacker comes short and the midfielder plays over the top, the attack never has a chance to get started.

VARIATIONS

- The defense adopts a different posture with each repetition. Instruct them to either press up high or drop off. Now the players must read in the flow of the game where the space will open. The striker should demand the ball either to his feet or in behind, making a verbal and also a physical gesture to instruct his teammates as to the service he wants.

Quick Strike from the Midfield: 8 vs. 8 plus Goalkeepers to Goal (1)

Two teams of eight (playing 3-3-2) play for possession in a zone stretching the width of the field and 35 yards long. Teams have three passes to put the ball in behind the opposing team's back/cone line on gaining possession. If the ball is played in onside, one attacker can pursue the ball and go to goal. If the team does not play in behind in the first three passes, it can earn a point by connecting ten consecutive passes. Note that the goalkeepers should clean up any errant through-passes to help make a quality entrance pass necessary. Restarts come from the coach at the side of the grid.

COACHING POINTS

- The mindset of a quick attack out of a crowded midfield space.
- Looking to intercept a pass while facing forward and already knowing what to do with the ball before moving.
- Coordinating pressing to win the ball in tight space.
- Quick combinations that release pressure and aid the timing of the run in behind.
- Timing of runs in behind.
- Weight of through-pass.
- Finishing breakaways.

VARIATIONS

- Require a particular type of buildup or combination (i.e., 1-2) before the through-pass (may need to adjust the pass limit accordingly).
- Require a through-pass from or to a particular player or position.
- One defender can chase the attacker to goal.

Quick Strike from the Midfield: 8 plus 1 vs. 8 plus 1 and Goalkeepers to Goal (2)

Place a defender in the *D* (the top of the 18-yard box) on each end. This player is activated when the through-pass is made. Two attackers are released with the through-pass, creating a 2 vs. 1 to goal.

Counterstrike: 7 vs. 7 plus Goalkeepers With Defenders Absent

This game and the exercise that follows allow the coach to create numbers-up situations within the game to assess the ability of the players to read and take advantage of counterattacking opportunities. Play 7 vs. 7 plus goalkeepers (1-3-3-1). Play without restrictions to establish the game and then instruct the teams that whenever the opposing goalkeeper touches the ball, two of their backs must run around any of the cones along the touchline. In the interim, play commences, granting the opponent a chance to counterattack against a temporarily depleted back line.

COACHING POINTS

- Recognize the transitional moment (when the goalkeeper receives the ball) and the opportunity to run and play forward quickly. What specific runs will be needed? Where should the ball be played to give the best chance of a quick attack without turning it over right away?
- This is a great opportunity to work with the goalkeeper on his decision-making in transition. Can he pick out the best target and distribute well and consistently to spur the team's counterattacking?

VARIATIONS

- Utilize a different cue and/or different players to initiate the coming and going of defenders. For instance, two midfielders from the defending team must run around a cone when a midfielder with the attacking team receives the ball. This variation will curb the attackers' ability to hoof the ball forward but still give them room to play forward through the midfield.

Neymar leads Paris St. Germain forward on the counterattack against Thomas Mueller and Bayern Munich.

Numbers Up! Assessing Counterattacking Prospects When the Ball Is Won

This is a standard playing environment featuring 7 vs. 7 plus goalkeepers. Each player on each team is assigned a number (one to seven). When the ball is turned over in the run of play, the coach calls out a number of a player on the defending team, and that player must instantly sit down and remain inactive until the ball leaves play or possession is won by the defending team. In the example above, the yellow left back has just sat down, leaving his team with a hole in its back line that the opponent attempts to exploit with a ball in behind.

COACHING POINTS

- This exercise is about the recognition of attacking opportunities. Quite often when possession is won, the opponent will be unbalanced in some way, and the team must quickly diagnose and exploit any opening. After playing for a few minutes, tell the teams to huddle and talk about how various openings should be exploited.

For example, if a holding midfielder sits down, there will be space in front of the opposing back line where a counterattack can be built. Conversely, if the defenders lose their lone attacker, there will be time and space to organize at the back, but longer balls forward may not be immediately available. Regardless, the team must learn to communicate the options to the player in possession so that coordinated attacking can be quickly organized.

- Similarly, do players off the ball recognize the right runs when the ball is won? If an opposing back sits down but the striker decides to check underneath rather than getting into the open space, the team will not attack in an efficient manner.

VARIATIONS

- The coach can call out multiple numbers. This is particularly useful when playing with larger numbers (i.e., 11 vs. 11) so that space can be opened quickly.

- The players compelled to sit down are only out for a brief moment (i.e., 5 seconds) to emphasize the need to counterattack quickly.

WHEN IT'S *NOT ON*: COACHING CONSIDERATIONS IN POSITIVE TRANSITION

One of the assumptions this study rests on is that there are counterattacking options available. It is important, for the sake of clarity and completeness, for the coach to ask and answer the question, "What if the counterattack is not on?" Depending on numerous factors, the attack can be unavailable from the outset or the attack can break down and be frustrated at almost any point.

Which factors determine when the counterattack is not on?

- Team disposition. If the team is coming out of a defending posture and is exhausted and/or team shape is distorted, there may be no opportunity to counterattack, and the team will need to build up slowly to compose itself (ideal) or to simply hoof the ball long to clear its lines and move the game forward, albeit with more defending on the horizon.

- Opponent disposition. When playing against a conservative, well-organized opponent, the team may find that it is simply too risky to thunder forward against a compact defending group, and the team may need to slow play and build up to attack goal. Part of the challenge in a game like this, incidentally, is to find moments to counterattack the opponent in the rare situation when they are out of balance and unprepared to defend. Interestingly, this type of opponent occasionally prompts a coach to encourage spirited attacking to try to open up the game, hoping the opponent will be emboldened to counterattack, which in turn may leave them unbalanced in transition when they lose the ball. Counter the counterattackers, so to speak.

Sergio Busquets of FC Barcelona, the consummate holding midfielder, turns the ball back against AS Roma in UEFA Champions League play.

- Opponent pressure. If the opponent presses and successfully gets numbers around the ball, forcing the player in possession to hold the ball or play backward, the moment for the counterattack may pass, forcing the team to break pressure with short passing and develop an indirect attack.
- Development of the counterattack. The attack can break down at any point, and players must learn to recognize when to pull the ball back and organize for an indirect attack. For instance, if the ball is moved quickly through the midfield, but the opponent manages to organize six players behind the ball and only two attackers join the counterattack, the attack will most often be thwarted, and the attackers, in most such circumstances, will be well advised to hold the ball and allow the team to move forward in support.
- Match situation. There may be match situations when counterattacking is not desirable, and the team must be coached to recognize when to play indirectly as well. For instance, a team that is bunkered into a defending posture with a narrow, late lead against a superior opponent may want to either limit the number of players free to go forward, or abolish counterattacking altogether in favor of keeping numbers behind the ball.
- Team philosophy. Some teams, for instance those lacking quick, attacking-minded players, simply do not have it in their DNA to be counterattacking oriented, and the coach may dictate that the group try to go forward quickly only in rare circumstances. Similarly, the attacking philosophy of the coach is an important factor in deciding how much counterattacking, if any, is permissible. Some coaches find wide open, counterattacking soccer to be aesthetically unpleasing, or believe that only possession-oriented soccer is "good soccer," and as a result they eschew counterattacking in style and design. Indeed, this philosophical jousting between the possession-oriented types and the wide-open attacking-style coaches is one of the enduring, entertaining coaching discussion topics. The Guardiola era at Barcelona gave the possession-oriented, indirect-attacking proponents much grist for their mill, though the success of Jurgen Klopp's Borussia Dortmund and, now, Liverpool teams has given the pressing/counterattacking clique its own argument.

It should be said that there is thankfully much middle ground here, and the coach must simply be aware of the continuum and communicate the team's philosophy with the players so that a common philosophy is on display on the field.

Xabi Alonso of Bayern Munich pulls the ball back to organize an indirect attack against the pressure of Borussia Moenchengladbach.

The ultimate message here is that every team will find at times that counterattacking is not the best option, and coaches must help their players and teams select the proper times and means to go forward quickly and also the times to settle down and bring the team forward in a more indirect posture.

Vertical Zones: Changing the Point of Attack After Winning Possession

In an 11 vs. 11 game on a full pitch, divide the playing area into four vertical zones. Require that all goals come from counterattacks and that those attacks be driven to goal through a zone other than the zone in which the attack started. This requirement will require the team to address both its shape and patterns of play. The team will understand that it must put players in the other zones and that those players must be incorporated for the team to score.

COACHING POINTS

- Team shape. Does the team address its shape on winning the ball by putting people in the other zones? Discuss the advantages of spreading players into different channels for counterattacking.
- Recognition. Is the player making the switch of play selecting the proper pass and timing?
- Execution. Does the team efficiently change zones and attack goal?
- Mentality. When the ball enters or leaves a zone, how do the players near and far away react? Do they push forward and help drive the team's attacks home?

VARIATIONS

- The coach calls out a signal for a sudden turnover. When the signal is given, the team in possession must immediately pass the ball to the nearest opponent. In this way, numerous, quick turnovers and counterattacks can be engineered.
- Time and/or pass number limits for the team in possession to force the team to attack the goal.
- Zone patterns that must be played to score. For instance, if the ball is won in a central zone, require that a cross be made from an outside zone.

Counterattacking Through Midfield Gates: Exploiting Wide Spaces

In an 8 vs. 8 plus goalkeepers game, place cone gates across the center line. Teams must attack through one of the gates on the counter. Each team plays 1-3-2-3, a formation that will create spaces along the back line to exploit. Allow each team a limited amount of time in possession (i.e., 12–15 seconds) to compel them to look to counterattack as fast as possible. In the example above, the goalkeeper distributes to the right back, who plays into the feet of the right forward. The right back then overlaps, and the forward plays through the gate to put the back up the line.

COACHING POINTS

- Spatial awareness. The shorter numbers in the midfield and on the back line will leave teams vulnerable on one flank or the other. If the defending team moves more players to the side where the ball is, it may be necessary to quickly change fields to exploit the space through the other gate. These spaces often open up in the full game in the same fashion.
- Speed and numbers in the counterattack. The attackers must recognize the space to attack and then get numbers into the pattern before the defenders can respond.
- Patterns of play. The pattern above is a common means of exploiting space on the flank, and other patterns should be imprinted on the team in training so that there is coordination on game day.
- Recognition. Why emphasize wide spaces for counterattacking? The use of wide spaces is less direct, but often safer, as teams often are more sensitive to protecting central areas.

VARIATIONS

- Require a certain pattern or that certain players be involved for the attackers to compel them to rehearse preferred movements and actions.
- Move the gates up the field to promote more width in the later stages of the counterattack.
- Remove the restriction on playing through the gates but offer a reward for utilizing passing through the wide areas (i.e., three points for a goal and one point for playing through a wide gate).

FOCUS ON SKILL: FINISHING

The ultimate stage of the counterattack is the opportunity to finish before goal. It matters little if a team creates dozens of scoring chances on the counter but cannot score when the opportunity is presented. Talented finishers are consistently in high demand at every level.

What skills are needed to finish in transition? Certainly, the ability to beat the goalkeeper 1 vs. 1 is mandatory. Relatedly, simple ball-striking before goal and under pressure will be required. Finally, finishing crosses with one's feet and one's head are also skills that must be rehearsed and sharpened.

As with most skills, finishing is necessarily not only technical, but also psychological. The best attackers are confident and look forward to the opportunity to bury a ball in the back of the net for their team.

The following exercises represent a selection of simple, efficient, and effective means of training finishing in environments that simulate opportunities that may appear in counterattacking in the game.

Harry Kane of Tottenham Hotspur scores against Aston Villa.

Blitz: Intensive Finishing—1 vs. Goalkeeper (1)

This environment makes for a progressive series of efficient finishing exercises. In the first stage, players start in short lines at opposite sides of the goals as pictured. They get eye contact with the goalkeeper and then take a setup touch before finishing. Then they retrieve a ball and get in line on the opposite end and wait for their turn to finish again.

COACHING POINTS

- Clean, consistent approach footwork and striking.
- Take a look at the goalkeeper after the setup touch. Shoot where the goalkeeper cannot save.
- Alternate the foot used to strike the ball. The shooters must be proficient with both feet.

Blitz: Intensive Finishing—1 vs. Goalkeeper—Breakaway (2)

This stage retains the same setup as the opening round, but now the attacker has the option to dribble the goalkeeper. The attacker can still shoot as well but must engage the goalkeeper through dribbling at him before finishing.

COACHING POINTS

- Speed. This training is realistic for both the attacker and the goalkeeper only if the attacker runs at speed throughout.
- Reading the goalkeeper. If possible, the shooter should finish while the goalkeeper is moving toward him, as it is very difficult for the keeper to move laterally while closing, and the shooter may catch the goalkeeper in midstep, which further complicates the attempt to save.

- Play simply. The tendency here for attackers is to want to chip the goalkeeper or execute a fancy move. Chipping at speed from this distance is a useful skill but most often the goalkeeper will stay close enough to his line where dribbling and drawing him out is the better bet. Fancy moves also tend to create more mistakes here, and if the goalkeeper gets closer to the attacker while the move is executed, the keeper's chances dramatically improve.

Blitz: Intensive Finishing—1 vs. 1 plus Goalkeeper (3)

Once again retaining the same setup, this stage creates repeated 1 vs. 1 opportunities to goal. The attacker must beat the defender on the dribble and then score past the goalkeeper. After being in the attacking role, the player then serves in the defender role for one turn for the next attacker starting on the opposite end. Players do not change ends in this exercise.

COACHING POINTS

- Changes of speed. The defender is arriving after just releasing or losing the ball and wants to slow down play. The attacker should try to change speeds and see if he can blow past the defender.
- Seek a good attacking angle. Young players tend to run out wide in the attacker role, trying to avoid the pressure of the defender. Any detour of this sort serves the defender and the goalkeeper's interests. Run at the defender and push behind him with a quick, short, sharp move, keeping to the central area before goal.
- Finishing. Once the defender is beaten, the attacker must put the ball behind the goalkeeper in consistent fashion.

Blitz: Intensive Finishing—2 vs. 1 plus Goalkeeper (4)

This stage creates repeated 2 vs. 1 (the defender is highlighted in red in the diagram) situations to goal. Two attackers must defeat the defender before finishing. Combination play (i.e., 1-2s, overlaps, etc.) should be emphasized. The last attacker to touch the ball becomes the defender for the next pair to attack in the other direction.

COACHING POINTS

- Speed and mobility in the attack. Young players tend to run straight ahead when they should get out of lanes and wrong-foot the defender by getting out of his vision.
- The player on the ball must commit the defender while the second defender creates a combination or through-pass angle.
- Direct running to goal at speed.
- Finishing. The result of the movement should be a 1 vs. goalkeeper look for the attackers, who must take their chances well.
- Both attackers should end up running to goal to bury any rebound or deflection.

Blitz: Intensive Finishing—3 vs. 2 plus Goalkeeper (5)

In the final stage, three attackers challenge two defenders and the goalkeeper. The last two attackers to touch the ball play defense for the next group of three to emerge from the bottom of the grid.

COACHING POINTS

- Speed of play. This is not a possession exercise, and the three attackers must press their attack home to goal as quickly as possible for this to be effective training for finishing counterattacks.

- Movement. Again, changing lanes, combination play, and penetrating will unbalance the defense.

- Finishing. The first good look in this instance should result in a goal. These opportunities must be finished in training so that the standard becomes that goals result from these looks on match day.

Robert Lewandowski of Bayern Munich finishes against Hannover 96.

Short Cross and Finish (1)

This environment is designed to give attackers intensive training in finishing crosses, with an eye toward improving technique and also confidence. A server sends in short crosses (adjust the width to suit the players and the exercise). Two runners arrive with the ball just beyond the 6-yard box to finish. Instruct the server to vary the timing and location of the serve to replicate different looks that will occur in the game. Note that the runners start from staggered sticks. The first runner should try to get across the face of the goal just beyond the 6-yard box. The second runner must hang back and finish anything that gets beyond the first runner. Instruct the goalkeeper to deal with any crosses inside the 6-yard box.

COACHING POINTS

- Mentality. Attackers closing the goal on crosses must be aggressive and determined to finish.
- Approach angles and timing. Although most often the timing will not be perfect on match day, the runners must learn to read the crosser to determine the best time to arrive so that they are not either standing and easily marked or late and miss their opportunity. Approach angle is also critical. Running into the path of the oncoming ball from an angle opposite the server creates a much longer finishing window than a run that just crosses over the path of the ball at a single point.
- Finishing technique. Whether the serve is on the ground or in the air, attackers must get comfortable regularly turning balls into the goal from this area.

VARIATIONS

- Keep track of score. Each pair gets a point for every first-time finish in front of goal.
- Add a recovering defender who runs with the attackers, trying to interfere with their finishing.
- Add movement for the server. The server dribbles to the end line from level with the penalty spot before serving. This added requirement helps the attackers time their runs to goal.

Transition Near Goal: 4 vs. 4 With Bumpers and Counter-attacking

Play 8 vs. 8 plus goalkeepers to full-sized goals in an area 44 yards by 30 yards (the width of the penalty area and an extra 12 yards in length). The game functions as 4 vs. 4 plus goalkeepers and bumpers. The team in possession can attack goal directly or play one of its bumpers and then go to the goal. Bumpers are limited to one touch and cannot shoot, enter play or be tackled. When a goal is scored, the team scoring the goal sprints back to its own goal and retrieves another ball before immediately attacking again. The team conceding the goal must change out its four field players, swapping positions with its bumpers. This is a fast-paced environment where there are many turnovers and sudden attacking opportunities as well as emergency defending situations.

COACHING POINTS

- Encourage players to be mindful of transition and how quickly the tactical needs of the situation can change. Can they read the play to determine what may happen next? How does their individual positioning and movement affect the play?
- One of the greatest benefits of this environment is the opportunity to encourage players to drive to the goal and to finish, even when there is just a brief attacking window. Players should develop confidence as they learn to recognize and exploit these chances.

VARIATIONS

- Limit the number of passes or touches for the active players to force them to attack the goal quickly and directly.
- Require a particular type of finish or sequence to score. For example, the attackers need a 1-2 or they must score off service from a bumper (to work on getting numbers to goal and finishing serves, if many of the team's counterattacks result in service).

7 vs. 7 plus Goalkeepers Functioning as 4 vs. 3 Transition

This is the same setup as the previous exercise except that the teams have seven players (plus goalkeepers) rather than eight. One team puts three players on the field, and the other puts four. Given the overload, both teams will have to adjust their tactics near the goal. The resting players serve as 1-touch bumpers on the attacking half perimeter for their teams. The coach times the activity, rotating the resting players every 90 seconds. The rotation reverses the overload to favor the other team.

COACHING POINTS

- The mismatched sides should produce rapid, open play. Encourage both teams to think and talk about their priorities. The team of three may want to try to attack very quickly when possible, before its opponents can get their superior numbers behind the ball. The team of four may find that it can force the ball to goal using its extra player. How quickly can they score?

6 vs. 6 plus Goalkeeper: Functional Counterattacking in the Front Third

This environment allows the coach to look at both the ball-winning and counterattacking of the midfield and forward group in a functional setting. Restarts come from the goalkeeper. The group defending the full-sized goal tries to score in the small goals for a point. They must get beyond the yellow cone line before finishing. The group of six attacking the large goal presses and when it wins the ball, it must immediately go to goal. Limit the counterattackers to four passes or 10 seconds to score. This restriction creates more repetition in winning the ball and going to goal, as well as providing realistic limits on the time available for a fast counterattack.

COACHING POINTS

- Team shape. The group of six attacking the large goal should be coached to channel the ball into areas (see above) and patterns that allow its teammates to intercept passes.
- Transition. How quickly can the group of six attacking the large goal get to goal when the ball is won? Often in these situations, the player winning the ball will be in position to drive to goal or push forward and serve into the box, and the team must be prepared to attack quickly and with numbers.
- Mentality. By reputation, the average forward dislikes defending. However, the opportunity to win the ball close to the opposing goal and to confront a defense that is stretched out and possibly unprepared should provide adequate incentive for attackers to press with energy and consistency.

VARIATIONS

- Require a certain type of counterattack (i.e., must score off a cross) from the group attacking the full-sized goal.
- Add players to create more realistic and complicated playing environments.

Real Madrid Head Coach Zinedine Zidane (right) and Cristiano Ronaldo

THE ANATOMY OF COUNTERATTACKING: CHOREOGRAPHING A SAMPLE PATTERN

This section will examine how to put all the training for counterattacking into a realistic, choreographed example to help players transfer principles emphasized in training to match situations.

Standard Team Formation: 1-4-2-3-1

Any standard movement stems from the team's standard formation, in this case a 1-4-2-3-1. For counterattacking purposes, this system has the following characteristics and benefits.

- Four players on the back line allow for width in defending.
- Two holding players who help protect the critical space in front of the center backs.
- Wing attackers and defenders who can get forward together and overwhelm opposing outside backs.
- A triangle midfield that can outnumber opponents playing a 1-4-4-2 and that can (with inter-passing) usually break pressure from an opponent when the ball is won in the center of the field.
- A playmaker at the top of the triangle who has the tactical flexibility to be difficult to mark in transition.
- A single target player who can roam against the opposing back line, making deep, wide, or underneath runs.

The Ball Is About to Be Won in the Back Third: Team Shape

With the team in good defensive shape, the opponents try an ill-advised long pass from their right back in to their center forward, who has come underneath the back line. The target team holding midfielder reads this pass and steps in front to win the ball.

This is a prime example of a situation where it is fairly clear that the ball will be won, and the team can already begin to think in terms of a counterattack. While defensive duties remain the primary consideration for all those players on the back line and in the midfield, note that the center forward has started to move off the opposing back line, and he is looking to find a lane through which he can be available to serve as an outlet. His movement underneath appears to be the best choice because it is likely that there will be pressure on the ball when it is won.

The Ball Is Won: First Moves

When the holding midfielder wins the ball, the team simultaneously moves to both solidify possession and also look to counterattack. The goalkeeper's mind-set shifts from guarding the goal and organizing the defense to supporting the team in possession and eyeing quick and long distribution to jump-start a counterattack. The center backs drop off, anticipating that if the ball-winner is turned back, they can serve as pressure release points. The wing backs step wider, dragging wing attackers away from their defensive bloc and/or opening up to receive. The other holding midfielder makes a snap judgment whether he must get under the ball (if there is forward pressure) or if he should open up forward, as he has done here. The attacking midfielder must decide whether to help release pressure or get forward. He has opted to stay put here, which draws the attention of the opposing holding midfielder. The wing attackers, as soon as they are sure the ball will be or has been won, look to stretch the team's shape wide and forward. Finally, the target player has continued his run into underneath space, as the ball-winner is under pressure. His angled run underneath pulls him away from the opposing back line, and the holding midfielder and also creates a clear window in which he can receive from the ball-winner.

Lay-Off and Hard Running Forward

The checking target player receives the pass from the holding midfielder and is pressurized by the opposing left center back, who steps off the back line to try to keep him from turning and to thereby stifle the counterattack. The attacking midfielder spins off his opposite number and into the space underneath the target player. The lay-off pass defeats the effort of the center back to try to prevent the turn by giving the ball to a playmaker who is faced up with the attacking goal. Note the early and hard running by the wing players and the follow-up supporting runs of all the players underneath the ball.

Penetrating Long Pass with Runs in behind the Defense

The team must think in terms of playing forward after the lay-off pass if the momentum of a fast counterattack is to be sustained. The attacking midfielder has numerous supporting options but is faced up, without forward pressure and with a number of penetrating runs developing. He opts to play the right wing in behind, knowing that the run of the center forward will mean that he will also be able to support the winger when he gets on the ball.

It is important to note here that players need to make constant and good decisions regarding the best way forward through this transition. It may be that the player in possession should continue to dribble for longer than planned because a target has drifted offside, or the opponent simply fails to get any pressure to the ball and other options forward are marked up. Thus, as coaches implement patterns for counterattacking, it's important to help the players understand the imperative to recognize the best options and have the freedom to improvise when necessary.

Changing the Point and Finishing

In the final slide, the defense has responded to the counterattackers' penetrating pass by rallying toward the right forward, who is now confronted by the left back and two more recovering defenders. Crucially, the opposing right back has also tucked in, concerned about the danger on the ball side of the field and the large gap between himself and the center back. The right forward, in possession, recognizes the need to change the point of the attack, and his early cross behind the defense frees up the left forward to finish the counterattack.

Counterattacking creates a series of decision-making moments that can be rehearsed with the thought that though every situation will be different, if players recognize important cues, successful patterns and common thinking will evolve. For instance, combining the requirements of certain exercises (i.e., changing the point of attack game presented earlier in this chapter) can condition players to perform the correct movements and techniques in this stage of the counterattack pattern.

German national team goalkeeper Laura Benkarth starts the counterattack.

THE GOALKEEPER AND POSITIVE TRANSITION

Just as the goalkeeper's role in negative transition involves both direct action (controlling the space behind the back line) and leadership (assessing threats and organizing the defense), her participation in positive transition often means starting the counterattack and also pushing the team forward.

The goalkeeper's ability to distribute quickly, accurately, and to the proper player can be critical to team success. One is immediately reminded of Tim Howard's distribution to Landon Donovan in the dying moments of the World Cup match against Algeria in 2010. A few seconds later, Donovan had buried a shot in the Algerian goal, propelling the United States into the Round of 16. Had Howard been any less proficient in his assessment of the counterattacking possibilities, his selection of target or his execution of the throw, the counterattack almost certainly would not have come off, and the United States might not have advanced.

Although it's less obvious, the goalkeeper also has a role in moving the team up the field with the advent of positive transition. Whether the transition begins with the goalkeeper or further up field, the goalkeeper must recognize and assist the team's movement forward by moving up the field and maintaining contact with the back line, which he must also push into the attack. Indeed, the goalkeeper's ability to create and control space in behind the forward-pushing defense will facilitate the inclusion of more players in the counterattack and relatedly give the team a better shape for maintaining possession if the counterattack breaks down.

8 vs. 8 plus Goalkeepers: Counterattacking From the Goal (1)

Play 8 vs. 8 (each team plays 1-3-3-2) plus goalkeepers on a full field and to full-sized goals. Encourage the goalkeepers to play early and forward in transition when the longer distribution is on. Early on (5 minutes) in the scrimmage, reward points only for playing the ball in to the opposing goalkeeper when the team has the ball in the front half of the field. This condition will put more balls in the goalkeepers' possession, setting the tone and repeating the transition opportunity. After 5 minutes, remove the condition, but state that shots on goal can only happen when all eight field players for a given team are in the front half of the field. Playing with this restriction creates better opportunities for the goalkeeper to get the team out on the counterattack, as there will be room in behind the opposing back line as they push forward. If the goalkeepers are not getting enough opportunities from the established scrimmage, the coach can also limit passes or time before shots must be taken. Finally, the coach can simply randomly call for turnovers through-passes to the opposing goalkeeper by the team in possession. With this last restriction, force the team ceding possession to all enter the front half of the field before it can recover and defend so that the counterattacking team can take advantage of the temporary imbalance of the defenders.

COACHING POINTS

- The recognition by the goalkeeper of counterattacking options. If the goalkeeper habitually rolls the ball out to a back when he could throw or kick to an open striker, freeze the game and point out the options forward. It is the prerogative of the coach as to the distribution priorities, but the goalkeeper should learn to read his options and understand the opportunities available through quick, calculated distribution of the ball.

8 vs. 8 plus Goalkeepers: Counterattacking from the Goal (2)—Goalkeeper Pushing Team Forward

An additional point of emphasis in this setting can be the goalkeeper pushing the counterattack forward. As the diagram above demonstrates, the goalkeeper can move forward to maintain good contact with his back line. As he moves, he is able to add more support to the attack in the form of more players running forward, while also protecting against a counterattack by sewing up the space in behind the back line as they move forward. The goalkeeper's actions also inspire confidence in the back line, as his presence helps them focus on potential opportunities and issues in front of them, rather than behind. Finally, the team moving forward often leaves opposing attackers in an offside position, should the other team gain possession and look to counterattack.

David de Gea of Manchester United urges his team forward.

Chapter 6

TRANSITION WITH THE WHISTLE

In researching and formulating the course of this book, one of the recurrent themes in discussions with colleagues was the notion that so much of transition is mental, and that by extension, some of the transition can be construed to be outside of the run of play because there is still a seminal moment where a game can be lost or won. For example, how many times do teams concede a set-piece, fail to adequately prepare and react to the moment, and lose? Conversely, many of the most effective teams seem to rise to the moment when a free kick is won and go on to win the match.

This chapter reviews many of the key moments where the game hangs in the balance with a decision that stops play and awards possession to one team. The essential challenge for the coach is in both planning (players must understand their individual and collective assignments in every set-piece) and execution. Indeed, this latter element is the most challenging. Players tend to relax with the whistle, often failing to make or track runs or finish or clear a serve. It is the stop-start nature of set-pieces and referee decisions that makes the mental transition so challenging to train.

FREE KICKS

Bayern Munich defends a Borussia Dortmund free kick: sharp mental transition from the run of play to defending or attacking set-pieces can be the difference in a tight match.

Watch any high-level match today, and it becomes very clear that teams place a high priority on drawing and taking advantage of free kicks. Every team has free-kick specialists who can bend a ball over a wall and past a goalkeeper or drop a long ball from near midfield onto the feet or head of a target near the goal. Teams also have intricate set plays requiring timed runs, split-second decisions, and technical precision from multiple players. Similarly, teams defending free kicks have carefully delineated defensive responsibilities for every player on the field, which must be executed in a timely, decisive manner.

When the whistle blows, both teams must react quickly to the transition to a free-kick situation. It's also worth noting here that attacking teams in particular tend to distort their team shape in response to a free-kick opportunity in the front third. Often, tall center backs are sent forward into the 18-yard box to try to win an aerial duel before goal while players less noted for their play in the air are sent back to midfield to cover on defense. This situation inherently requires extra concentration and awareness from both teams, as the attackers must worry about being countered if they don't score, and the defenders must turn an eye toward getting out on the counter when they win the ball, hoping to catch their opponents in poor defending posture.

The following exercise allows the coach to work on the key transitional moments of taking free kicks and also trying to get out on the counter (or prevent the counter) after defending a free kick.

Free Kick and Counter

This exercise can be run using varied numbers. One team practices taking free kicks from various distances and angles. The coach can use this part of the setup to imprint free-kick plays and tendencies. After each kick, the other team practices immediate counterattacks in transition. The team defending the counters should leave a pair of defenders near its goal (here the starting point is the center line) and have a recovering player(s) to try to stop the counterattacks. The teams should frequently change roles.

COACHING POINTS

- Free-kick plays and/or defending free kicks. The ability to give the players concentrated training in attacking and defending free kicks is a point of emphasis here.
- Mentality and patterns for counterattacking after free kicks. Because opponents will send numbers forward (and often send their tallest, often central, defenders), their shape for defending counterattacks in these situations is almost always very inadequate. Thus, the team must get out quickly on the counter and drive attacks to the goal.

VARIATIONS

- Tinker with the number of attackers and defenders for the counterattack phase to create dynamic training.
- Limit the number of passes for the counterattacking team before it scores to force it to go immediately to goal.
- Limit the amount of time available to the counterattacking team to compel it to immediately go to goal.
- Allow the free kick team to try to score if it breaks up the counterattack (counter the counterattack).

Danish players defend a corner kick vs. Finland.

CORNER KICKS

There is continuing debate among coaches as to the import of corner kicks in a team's attacking strategy. For years, it was assumed that the ability to pack the box with players (above) would inevitably create more goal scoring. In recent years, many coaches have de-emphasized the utility of lobbing or driving corner kicks into the box, opting instead to send multiple players to the corner, take a short kick or pass, and simply restart possession.

Statistics seem to favor the latter approach, with studies usually recording just 2–5 percent as a success rate for scoring off corner kicks. That said, some teams opt to go short on the corner, in part, because they have few tall players to finish serves into the box or because the game situation merits keeping possession (i.e., the team is playing with a lead late in the match). Regardless, there is no denying that mentality and concentration play a huge role in corner kicks. Players have a tendency to relax after the whistle is blown, and mental errors on the defensive side of the ball have produced many goals. Similarly, teams that tend to score more often on attacking corner kicks often adopt the mentality that they are committed to scoring from their set plays, and the edge they gain from this approach plays a role in their success.

Corner-Kick Machine

This is a game based on corner-kick restarts that the coach can use to train the team to prepare to take and defend corner kicks. Teams alternate serving from opposite corners. The coach can implement and rehearse specific plays or set and tweak the defending posture of the team. Play to a set number of goals or clearances. It is important to note that this game should only be played for a few minutes, as the repetition can have the effect of dulling the mental sharpness of the players, which will defeat the purpose.

COACHING POINTS

- In this case, the major point of emphasis is mental sharpness, in regard to the attacking side. Coach the setup, the service and the quality of the runs, as well as the aggression required of the group. They must be hungry to get the first touch on the serve and to finish. In regard to the defenders, coach their shape, check to see that they cover their defensive responsibilities, especially their determination to get the first touch and to clear the ball from the area.

RED CARD

As the photo above indicates, red-card sanctions can sew havoc among the players on the field. Earned or not, the issuing of a red card places one team at a severe disadvantage, while immensely benefiting the other, for the balance of the match. Indeed, preparing the team to cope with the missing player and the mental stress associated with the absence is critical to the team's ability to transition through this moment in the match, and it can be dealt with in similar fashion to an injury to a key player.

Players' response to going down (or up) must be conditioned through training. The team must quickly process and set aside its collective frustration in favor of answering the question, "Now what?" Depending on the match situation and the player lost, both teams must immediately move to cope with the new tactical requirements.

11 vs. 10 Training Match With Red Card

In a training match with full-sided teams, issue a red card for a foul. The coach can quietly prearrange a foul (make sure no one is hurt!) or an argument to create a more realistic scenario if desired. As with the injury scenario, see how the teams react. Do the remaining players come together to discuss the implications? Are the players on the affected team able to refocus? There is often a letdown after the team has lost a player in this fashion, and the team must be able to rally to continue the match to a successful conclusion.

COACHING POINTS

- The team that is now down a man: If the team is losing, how can they cope with the loss and battle back in the match? It may want to change its shape, depending on the time left in the match and its tactics, and it needs to find a rallying mentality in spite of the loss of its teammate. If the team has the lead, it must shake off the loss and figure out how to tactically cope with the demands of the match by dropping a player to a deeper position if needed and/or playing more directly to keep its opponents away from its goal.

- The team with the man advantage: If the team is losing, how does it now take advantage of the opponent, which is now down a man? Clearly, the best time to strike will be immediately, while its opponents are reeling from the referee's decision. Can it push another man forward? Should it try to serve deeper passes into its opponents' box to try to increase the pressure? If the team is leading, how can the loss of a player for its opponents help the team kill off the game? Should the team risk a bit to try to score again right away and put the match out of reach? Should it become more conservative, and knock the ball around, hoping to grind down its opponents by making them chase the game?

Once again, the answers to these questions should be known to the team and calmly discussed by the group on the field in training in preparation for match day.

VARIATION

- Issue red cards to multiple players, forcing the teams to reexamine their tactics and mind-set.

Idress Carlos Kameni of Malaga saves the penalty kick of Christiano Ronaldo (Real Madrid).

PENALTY KICKS

The decision to issue a penalty kick is one of the most influential made by game officials, and players from both teams frequently react sharply to the decision to award (or not grant) a kick from the spot. Much has been written in recent years regarding the strategy of taking and defending penalty kicks (particularly Ben Lyttleton's excellent *Twelve Yards*), and for the purposes of this study, the most relevant factor is the reaction of both teams to the call.

- For the defending team, the effort must quickly shift from questioning the call to preparing to defend the kick. Typically, several players do what they can to delay the kick and distract the kicker, from talking with the official or the player preparing to take the kick to muddling about with the ball in hand for a moment. Others must get the closest spots to goal as starting points (both ends of the D arc at the top of the 18-yard box). The defenders also want to talk in terms of recovering the rebound and building up their goalkeeper to make the save.

- For the attackers, it's about identifying the shooter and then clearing the deck, so to speak, for that player. They help coax opponents out of the box and then find good spots along the top of the 18-yard box from which to charge in and finish a rebound.

The outcome of the penalty effort will provide a psychological jolt to both teams, regardless of the outcome. If a goal is scored, the attackers celebrate, and the defenders mourn their bad fortune. If the penalty is missed or saved, the defenders receive a huge boost while the attackers feel immense disappointment. Teams must be prepared to carry on and seize these moments to turn the match in their favor.

Indeed, the transition back to the run of play from a saved penalty can be a crucial moment in the match. The defending team must get in and clear the ball, and because contingents of both teams gather around the 18-yard box for the kick, there may be a chance for the defenders to immediately counterattack. For the team taking the penalty, there is an inevitable sense of letdown from a miss, but there is still an opportunity to pounce on any rebound and finish, or reattain possession and continue attacking. At worst, the team must get back into good defensive shape and mentally move beyond the sense of disappointment.

Training Match with Penalty Kicks

The good news with regard to penalty kicks is that it is relatively easy to insert a spot kick into a training match every day at training. Making a phantom call to further stir the pot, mentally speaking, is good practice. Try to find a tense moment, often near the end of the training match, to make the call and assemble both teams around the area, just as in a regular match. Attaching incentives, such as cleaning-up equipment for the team that loses the match, also helps add to the moment. It is important to note that it is desirable to play on for a few minutes after the penalty try to monitor and then discuss both teams' reactions to the event.

Chapter 7

THE MENTAL GAME, DECISIVE MOMENTS—TRANSITION THROUGH TIME PHASES AND INCIDENTS IN THE MATCH

Continuing the theme of mental transition, it is clear that there are occurrences in the match that greatly affect the course of play and that players and teams must seize the opportunity granted by such happenings or be able to cope with a setback in order to maximize their performance. Similarly, there are situational phases where the match changes in nature (e.g., after a goal is scored). These transitional moments, while often surprising, can be rehearsed to prepare the team for match day.

Franck Ribery is helped off by Bayern Munich training staff.

PLAYER INJURIES

Over the course of a season, every team suffers injuries. Those injuries, particularly when they occur in the run of the match, can be decisive to the outcome of matches. There are many questions for the coach to ponder when a player is unable to continue.

1. Should the player be replaced? Where there are limited substitutions, a coach may need to ponder the need to play short for a time. If allotted substitutions have already been used, there is no choice, and the team must reshape and play on. If the player may be able to return after receiving attention, how long should the coach wait? If the injury occurs near halftime, can the team play short until the half ends to give the player more time to recover?

2. Which player should replace the injured team member? With each substitution, the team's make-up changes, and there is the possibility, or the requirement, to make tactical adjustments based on the match, the opponent, and the influence of the new player.

3. How does this substitution affect the overall match plan? Substitutions often have a ripple effect, as a change to one position, particularly where the substitutions are limited to three for the match at the professional level, may limit or compel other changes.

Once the injury has been assessed and the player replaced, the onus is on the team to adjust in the flow of the match. Often when a team suffers an injury to a key player, there is a collective letdown that is an opening for the opponent to seize control of the match. Players and teams must understand this danger and be prepared to react to overcome any concerns about the injured player's departure.

In general, player leadership is critical in this moment. Many teams gather on the field to talk about the anticipated change and build up their confidence and cohesion to continue.

To simulate this moment in training, try the following exercise.

11 vs. 11 Game With Injury to Key Player(s)

Play a training match with full sides. It is useful to create some tension by conditioning the match (i.e., one team leads with 10 minutes remaining). Talk with a key player before starting play, and instruct him to go down with an injury in the first minute. Remove the player from the field and then observe the reaction. Do the players on both teams gather to discuss how to change the game? The team that will be down a man should be arranging to cover his space, while its opponents should recognize and try to exploit the change in the opposing team's personnel and formation.

COACHING POINTS

- If the team that is winning is down a man, it needs to hunker down and kill the game. Which line is the missing player from? If he's a back, the team will certainly need to drop another player onto the back line. If he is a forward, the team must understand that there will be less pressure on the ball and fewer counterattack targets and play accordingly.

- If the team that has lost a man is down on the scoreboard, how should it try to find momentum? Again, if they have lost a forward, they need to push another man up top, whereas if it's a back-line player, they may just need to cope with the absence by playing more directly, which would be natural anyway when they are chasing the game.
- If the team that's winning observes that its opponent is down a man, how should it change tactics? It may be that they can knock the ball around a bit to help kill the game off with the opponent short a man. If the man can be replaced (i.e., in an unlimited substitution situation), how does the loss of the specific player affect the opponent?
- If the team that's losing sees its opponents lose a key player, how can it use the absence to its advantage? If the missing player is a tall center back, perhaps the opponents will be more vulnerable to crosses and balls served toward their box? If they have lost their midfield leader, perhaps building through that space will now become easier.

Regardless, the reaction needs to be a calm conversation among the team as to the changed tactical needs of the situation.

Borussia Dortmund coach Peter Bosz makes tactical adjustments as Mario Goetze is helped off by team trainers.

WEATHER

Weather: Roma vs. Sampdoria

One of the most challenging variables in many soccer matches is weather. Wind, rain, lightning, snow, cold, heat, darkness, and lousy pitch conditions all wreak havoc with tactical planning and can decisively affect the mentality of the teams playing the match. What's more, these conditions often set in over the course of a match, making the mental transition into these conditions an important consideration.

Over the course of a season, teams almost inevitably play in or through daunting weather conditions. The most prevalent issue in most areas is wind. The coach must decide before the match whether to try to take the wind or defer and enjoy the wind at the team's back in the second half. Even then, there is the possibility that the coin toss is lost, and one's preference is denied. There are a lot of variables as to whether a team tries to play with the wind either in the first or second half. Some teams start notoriously well or poorly, and it may be necessary to try to take the wind or defer based on the performance expectations for one's team.

Another factor is the tactical implications of the particular match. If one's team and the opponent both like to play indirectly and knock the ball around on the ground, the wind may not be much of a decisive factor. If, however, either team or both like to bang the ball all over the park in the air, the wind can be very destructive to tactical play, and the coach will have to decide whether there is an advantage to having or foregoing the wind in the first half. The other remarkable consideration regarding wind is the fact that it's very fickle. Wind tends to fade with the evening, but not always as predicted, and it has a funny way of turning around at the half.

Regardless, the important message here is that the team must be prepared to play through windy conditions. If the coach intends to play into the wind and bunker through the first 45 minutes, that message must be relayed to the team before the game, and players must understand the difficulty they will face early on. Conversely, if the coach decides to take the wind, the team must grasp the importance of playing to gain an advantage early on, because it may be difficult to carve out attacking opportunities into the wind later in the game. Rain, snow, and lousy field conditions all present similar decision-making opportunities for the coach, and the team must be prepared to embrace the match conditions.

The anticipation of bad weather and worsening field conditions merit special consideration. In youth soccer, games are often canceled or considered played if a portion of the match is completed before playing conditions become unsafe. Thus the coach must monitor conditions and prepare his team to gain an advantage in the portion of the match that is played. For instance, if a storm is anticipated in the second half and the match will be considered full if three-fourths of regular time is played, the team may need to transition in the course of the match from one playing style and psychological approach to another. If the team has a lead and only needs to play for another 10 minutes in heavy rain, the tactical approach may change to simply playing forward, and the mental approach may be one of killing off the match. If, however, the team is down and the match will be considered full in a few minutes, the transition may be to a preplanned aggressive attacking strategy involving serving balls into the box. Another important consideration is the possibility of weather-related delays (i.e., lightning). How will the team cope with the need to come out and play again after going to the locker room? Ultimately, it is important here that the coach adequately prepare his team to transition through weather conditions that impact the course of the match.

The collective argument that it is important to plan to play through difficult weather conditions represents the best rationale for training in challenging conditions. For years, World Cup champion coach Anson Dorrance carefully limited the maintenance of the training pitch for his women's team at the University of North Carolina because he wanted it to have to battle through tougher conditions in training than it would face on match day. Similarly, it will be useful for all teams to train in rain, mud, and wind to duplicate the most challenging of match-day weather conditions.

OGC Nice celebrates a goal in their Ligue 1 match against Olympique Lyon.

TWILIGHT

The majority of goals are scored in a phase coaches call "twilight," which encompasses the opening and closing 5 minutes of every half and also the 5 minutes after a goal is scored.

The opening 5 minutes tend to see nervy touches and a lack of mental sharpness from players finding their mental way into the game, and many coaches adopt conservative tactics to open the half, playing directly into their opponents' half just to keep the ball away from their goal until everyone has settled in.

Similarly, the closing 5 minutes of the half will always feature tired players, who know that they are nearing the break or the end of the match. Minds wander, nerves jangle, and mistakes are made.

When a goal is scored, there is a letdown for the team conceding (see body language in the photo above) and euphoria for the team that scores. The upshot is that both teams' mental states are transitioned away from focus within the run of play, and there is greater likelihood of mistakes leading to goals.

Again, for the purposes of this study, the important factor is that the move through any twilight period in the match poses a mental transition that the team can prepare to exploit.

Conditioning Scrimmage to Train for Twilight Phase

This is a series of brief 11 vs. 11 games designed to prepare the team to deal with the twilight phase. The coach can introduce a variety of conditions to simulate twilight phases.

EXAMPLES:

- Opening 5 minutes of the match. Adjust the tactics of both teams to reflect the situation. For example, utilize a standard kick-off play and then play conservatively along the back line, passing long to avoid playing in the team's back third for 5 minutes. As a related strategy, also try to play to the strikers' feet and then push the ball deep, hoping to put the opponent on the defensive and under pressure near his goal.

- Five minutes after a goal is scored. When one team scores, again adjust tactics and set the mental priorities for both teams. Begin with a kickoff and play for 5 minutes. Many coaches like to incentivize their teams by offering a reduction in fitness training or added fitness training based on the team's performance in this pressure situation. Although coaching schools caution that this type of parameter gives fitness a negative connotation, it is nonetheless a useful way to produce more intensity.

- The final 5 minutes of the period. The only way to simulate this transition is to play for a while (15–20 minutes minimum) and then announce the amount of time remaining. The coach can also tweak the game by adjusting the score or other variables (i.e., take a man off for one team) to add more mental pressure to the situation. The idea is to try to replicate a situation where players are tired and where the game is on the line. How will they respond, particularly knowing that this is a dangerous or potentially rewarding phase?

This type of scrimmage setting is ideal for imprinting on players the risks and rewards of playing through these transitional phases of the match and also the tactical tendencies that the coach wishes to stress on match day.

PLAYING WITH A LEAD

Playing up a goal, particularly late in the match, can be as nerve-racking as playing from down a goal, as the opponent ratchets up the pressure, throwing increasing numbers forward and serving balls into your box at every opportunity. Set-pieces, too, become even more tense, as more players are shuttled into the box to try to finish corners, free kicks, and long throws.

The response to these increased efforts by the opponents must be firm psychological steadfastness across the team and tactical adjustments that can be made on the fly as the game winds down. Tactically, many teams change personnel and tactics with a lead late. If the formation is changed, it is usually to withdraw a forward and add a player on the back line. This adjustment not only thickens the back wall against all the aerial serves and crosses that are being tossed in but also reduces the pressure that can be applied to those serves by your own attackers.

Additional tactics by teams in the lead include the following:

- Slowing the game down at set-pieces by walking, pulling up socks, fronting the ball, and so forth.
- Committing professional fouls to disrupt the other team's momentum.
- Making substitutions to slow the game.
- Playing the ball long and out of play at every opportunity.
- Shielding the ball in the attacking corners of the field.

Once again, the team must exercise these tactics in a unified and coherent manner, as it just takes one player missing an assignment to create an opportunity for the opponent to break through and score.

FC Barcelona's Marc-Andre ter Stegen and his teammates fight off a late surge from Spanish foes Sevilla FC.

Conditioning Game to Train Playing With a Lead

The red team above is playing with five across the back and a single front-runner. The right back has just lobbed a long pass into the attacking corner, and the white team will have to start forward from deep as time drains away. The coach can use brief, 10-minute games like this to rehearse tactics for protecting the lead late in the match.

Arturo Vidal of Bayern Munich protects the ball and the lead (3–1) against Paris-St. Germain in UEFA Champions League play in 2017.

PLAYING FROM BEHIND

Playing down a goal is one of the most difficult coaching scenarios in soccer. With no time-outs and limited lineup change possibilities at the highest levels, the challenge is to rally one's team while the game carries on. Trailing by a goal is especially daunting as the match winds down, as the opponent typically resorts to killing off the game by dragging out every possible second from each restart, fouling and milking injuries to disrupt the game and spraying the ball all over the park whenever they touch it.

That said, the trailing team must have a collective understanding of the tactical and psychological requirements of mounting a successful comeback. On the psychological side, the team must be able to focus amid all the tactics practiced by the leading team. Many teams lose their composure and commit silly fouls while trailing, which further compounds both the time issue and the collective frustration. The players must rally one another, pushing through the frustration to create chances and continually restart buildups to goal.

Tactically, trailing teams often change formations, moving a player off the back line and into the midfield or onto the front line. This alteration usually indicates a shift to more direct play, with lots of serves into the opponents' box. Relatedly, the team becomes more vulnerable to counterattacks, and the back-line players have to play with desperation to get the ball forward. The crucial conclusion here is that the team must be *prepared* and have a common understanding as to what will transpire when the team is trailing.

Jamie Vardy's (right) late heroics frequently rally Leicester City (seen here vs. FC Copenhagen).

Conditioning Game to Train Playing From Behind

Here, the white team has removed a defender and added a frontline player. Its goalkeeper, playing very high up field, prepares to loft a ball into the opposing box. Short training games like this can be used to imprint late game tactics for trying to play from behind.

OTHER CHALLENGES

There are myriad other issues that can influence the team's performance and the flow of the match. Human distractions are a common challenge to a team's concentration. Occasionally an official will call a match that keeps one or both teams off-balance (i.e., by calling all kinds of mystery fouls or calling nothing at all). Opposing coaches can also be a nuisance, demonstrating along the touchline throughout the match and even engaging the opponent's players. Finally, there is always the likelihood of spectators distracting the team throughout the course of the match. Like the other transition requirements in this chapter, these elements can occur out of nowhere and be transient inside of the match. The only solace for the coach, as with the other challenges discussed here, is that it is possible to replicate and thereby address these distractions in training, helping the team understand how to deal with the extra variables on match day.

PENALTY-KICK SHOOT-OUT

Every manager would like to see the game concluded in 90 minutes. Because I don't think there's any way to prepare for penalty kicks. –Germany Coach Joachim Löw

While teams definitively train to compete in a penalty kick shoot-out, the results are often unreliable for predicting match-day performance because it is so difficult to replicate the conditions that typically accompany the shoot-out.

Shoot-outs typically happen at the conclusion of regular time and overtime (occasionally youth tournaments actually use shoot-outs in place of games to determine winners where weather and field conditions limit time for match play), meaning players are exhausted. Most often, injuries or other tactical requirements dictate that the group the coach would envision to take penalties may not be on the field. Spectator pressure, frustrations of the match, and sheer pressure to perform all weigh heavily on both the shooters and the goalkeeper. Consequently, it's typically the weaker team, if there is one, which gambles with its tactics and tries to play for a shoot-out.

Unquestionably, this is the ultimate test of mental transition in the match. Players go from giving their last drop of energy during the overtime periods to being required to take a spot kick with the game on the line. How can the team adequately prepare to transition and perform with all the variables in mind?

Eintracht Frankfurt players await the outcome of the final kick in a penalty shoot-out against Borussia Moenchengladbach in the DFB Cup semifinal match in 2017.

Mock Penalty-Kick Shoot-Out

This exercise is a framework for a mock-up of a penalty-kick shoot-out. First, run this game after a strenuous training session, preferably involving a lot of game play and fitness so that the players are fatigued. It is also important to provide unfamiliar opposition where possible. Perhaps another team from the club, or a junior varsity team, or a men's vs. a women's team. The unfamiliarity is critical because goalkeepers very quickly become accustomed to the habits of the shooters on their teams and they tend to stymy their own players, wrecking the shooters' confidence. Finally, provide as many details as possible that simulate match day, from coin tosses and scoreboards to long walk-ups (walk, don't run) for the shooters. It is also recommended that this practice be repeated on a weekly basis throughout the season and that the team try to have seven or more shooters who are ready to go on game day, as injuries and required substitutions may play havoc with the expected first five.

CONCLUSION

The purpose of this book has been to emphasize the importance of transitional moments in modern soccer. As the game continues to be played at increasing pace and as coaches and players improve their ability to recognize and embrace the advantages of mastering the transitional phases of the game, it appears that the current trends toward a faster game will continue for the foreseeable future. It is hoped that the ideas, thought processes, and training exercises presented in this book will be useful to coaches seeking to improve their teams' ability to transition.

Best wishes for your coaching,
Tony Englund and John Pascarella

SOURCES AND RECOMMENDED READING

INTERVIEWS

Casey Holm. Assistant Men's Coach, University of St. Thomas.

Mike Huber. Staff Coach, Sporting St. Croix Soccer Club.

Nathan Klonecki. Director of Coaching, Sporting St. Croix Soccer Club.

PRINT AND FIELD SESSIONS

Ancelotti, Carlo. *Quiet Leadership: Winning Hearts, Minds, and Matches.* Penguin, 2016.

______________. *The Beautiful Games of an Ordinary Genius.* Rizzoli, 2010.

Anderson, Chris and David Sally. *The Numbers Game: Why Everything You Know About Soccer is Wrong*. Penguin, 2013.

Arena, Bruce. *What's Wrong with US? A Coach's Take on the State of American Soccer After a Lifetime on the Touchline.* Harper, 2018.

Athanasios, Terzis. *Jurgen Klopp's Defending Tactics*. Soccer Tutor, 2015.

______________. Marcelo Bielsa: *Coaching Build Up Play Against High Pressing Teams.* Soccer Tutor, 2017.

Balague, Guillem. *Pep Guardiola: Another Way of Winning. The Biography.* Orion, 2012.

______________. *Brave New World: Inside Pochettino's Spurs*. Weidenfeld & Nicolson, 2017.

Bangsbo, Jens and Birger Peitersen. *Fitness Training in Soccer–A Scientific Approach.* Reedswain, 2003.

______________. *Defensive Soccer Tactics.* Human Kinetics, 2002.

Barker, Ian. Session presentations at the NSCAA Master Coach Certificate Course and the NSCAA/USC Conventions.

Barney, Andy. *Training Soccer Legends.* Soccer Excellence, 2006.

Bate, Dick and Ian Jeffreys. *Soccer Speed.* Human Kinetics, 2015.

_____________. *Coaching Advanced Soccer Players: 40 Training Games and Exercises.* Reedswain, 1999.

Beale, Michael. *The Socccer Academy: 100 Defending Practices and Small Sided Games.* Reedswain, 2007.

_____________. *The Soccer Academy: 140 Overload Games and Finishing Practices.* Reedswain, 2007.

_____________. *Training Creative Goalscorers.* World Class Coaching, 2008.

Beswick, Bill. *One Goal: The Mindset of Winning Soccer Teams.* Human Kinetics, 2016.

Bisanz, Gero, and Norbert Vieth. *Success in Soccer Volume 2: Advanced Training.* Phillipka-Sportverlag, 2002.

Blank, Dan. *High Pressure: How to Win Soccer Games by Smothering Your Opponent.* Dan Blank, 2017.

_____________. *Shutout Pizza: Smarter Soccer Defending for Players and Coaches.* Soccer IQ, 2014.

_____________. *Soccer IQ: Volume I.* Dan Blank, 2012.

_____________. *Soccer IQ: Volume 2.* Dan Blank, 2013.

Calvin, Michael. *Living on the Volcano The Secrets of Surviving as a Football Manager.* Century, 2015.

_____________. *No Hunger in Paradise.* Century, 2017.

Carson, Mike. *The Manager: Inside the Minds of Football's Leaders.* Bloomsbury, 2013.

Cox, Michael. The Mixer: The Story of Premier League Tactics from Route One to False Nines. Harper Collins, 2017.

Crothers, Tim. *The Man Watching: A Biography of Anson Dorrance*. Sports Media Group, 2006.

Cruyff, Johan. *My Turn: A Life of Total Football*. Nation Books, 2016.

Dicicco, Tony and Hacker, Colleen. *Catch Them Being Good*. Penguin, 2002.

Dorrance, Anson. *Training Soccer Champions*. JTC Sports, 1996.

Dost, Harry, Hans-Dieter te Poel and Peter Hyballa. *Soccer Functional Fitness Training*. Meyer & Meyer, 2016.

Dure, Beau. *Long-Range Goals: The Success Story of Major League Soccer*. Potomac Books, 2010.

Englund, Tony. *Goalie Wars! Goalkeeper Training in a Competitive Environment*. World Class Coaching, 2010.

______________. *Players' Roles and Responsibilities in the 4-3-3: Attacking*. World Class Coaching, 2011.

______________. *Players' Roles and Responsibilities in the 4-3-3: Defending*. World Class Coaching, 2011.

______________. *Style and Domination: A Tactical Analysis of FC Barcelona*. World Class Coaching, 2012.

______________. *The Art of the Duel: Elite 1 vs. 1 Training*. Foreword by Anson Dorrance. World Class Coaching, 2014.

______________. *Competitive Small Group Training: Maximizing Player Development in the Small Group Setting*. Foreword by Tony Sanneh. World Class Coaching, 2014.

______________. *Complete Soccer Coaching Curriculum for 3-18 Year Old Players Volume I*. NSCAA, 2014 (contributor).

______________, John Pascarella. *Soccer Goalkeeper Training: The Comprehensive Guide*. Meyer & Meyer, 2017.

Ferguson, Alex. Leading: *Learning from Life and My Years at Manchester United.* Hachette Books, 2015.

Franks, Ian and Mike Hughes. *Soccer Analytics: Successful Coaching Through Match Analysis.* Meyer & Meyer, 2016.

Gordon, Jon and Mike Smith. *You Win in the Locker Room First.* Wiley, 2015.

Gregg, Lauren. *The Champion Within: Training for Excellence.* JTC Sports, 1999.

Harrison, Wayne. *Soccer Awareness: Developing the Thinking Player.* Reedswain.

______________. *Coaching the 4-2-3-1.* Reedswain.

______________. *Coaching the Flex 1-3-3-1-3.* Reedswain, 2015.

______________. *The Art of Defending, Parts I and II.* Reedswain, 2002.

______________. *Recognizing the Moment to Play.* Reedswain, 2002.

______________. *Game Situation Training for Soccer.* Reedswain, 2005.

Honigstein, Raphael. *Das Reboot: How German Soccer Reinvented Itself and Conquered the World.* Nation Books, 2015.

______________. *Bring the Noise: The Jurgen Klopp Story.* Nation Books, 2018.

Hyballa, Peter and Hans-Dieter te Poel. *German Passing Drills.* Meyer & Meyer, 2015.

Jankowski, Timo. *Successful German Soccer Tactics: The Best Match Plans for a Winning Team.* Meyer & Meyer Sport, 2015.

Jones, Robyn with Tom Tranter. *Soccer Strategies: Defensive and Attacking Tactics.* Reedswain, 1999.

Kouns, Chris. *Counter Attacking in the Modern Game.* World Class Coaching, 2016.

Lloyd, Carli. *When Nobody was Watching: My Hard-Fought Journey to the Top of the Soccer World.* Houghton Mifflin Harcourt, 2016.

Lucchesi, Massimo. *Pressing*. Reedswain, 2003.

Luxbacher, Joseph A. *Attacking Soccer: Tactics and Drills for High-Scoring Offense*. Human Kinetics, 1999.

Lyttleton, Ben. *Twelve Yards: The Art and Psychology of the Perfect Penalty Kick*. Penguin, 2014.

Meyer, Urban. *Above the Line: Lessons in Leadership and Life from a Championship season*. Penguin, 2015.

Neveling, Elmar. *Jurgen Klopp: The Biography*. Ebury Press, 2016.

Perarnau, Marti. *Pep Confidential: The Inside Story of Pep Guardiola's First Season at Bayern Munich*. Arena, 2014.

______________. *Pep Guardiola: The Evolution*. Arena, 2016.

Pascarella, John. Field session, 2016 NSCAA Convention.

______________. Field and Classroom presentations, NSCAA Master Coach Certificate, 2015.

Rivoire, Xavier. *Arsene Wenger: The Biography*. Aurum, 2007.

Roscoe, Phil and Mike Vincent. *Modern Attacking & Goal Scoring*. World Class Coaching, 2010.

Tipping, Jeff. *Drills and Exercises to Develop the Elite American Player*. Jeff Tipping, 2012.

______________. Session presentations at the NSCAA Conventions.

Tsokaktsidis, Michail. *Coaching Transition Play*. Soccer Tutor, 2017.

Verheijen, Raymond. *Conditioning for soccer*. Reedswain, 1998.

Walker, Sam. *The Captain Class: The Hidden Force that creates the World's Greatest Teams*. Random House, 2017.

West, Phil. *I Believe that We will Win: The Path to a US Men's World Cup Victory*. Overlook, 2018.

Wilson, Jonathan. *Inverting the Pyramid: A History of Football Tactics*. Orion Books, 2008.

CREDITS

Design & Layout

Cover and interior design: Annika Naas

Layout: Amnet Services

Art & Photos

Cover and interior photos: © dpa

Interior illustrations: Sports-Graphics, www.easy-sport-software.com

Editorial

Managing Editor: Elizabeth Evans

Copyediting: Amnet Services

What leading soccer coaches and educators are saying about *Soccer Transition Training: Moving Between Attack and Defense* by Tony Englund and John Pascarella.

"I am delighted to be able offer an endorsement to this important contribution to coaching education. Tony and John are friends, and they are great professionals. Moreover they share a passion for sharing their ideas and presenting them in a contextual and applicable way. The work of Tony and John is sound in both theory and practice because they work daily in the applied world of the coach supporting youth athletes through to pro athletes.

The topic of transition is among the most popular for coaches to consider and discuss and also one of the most difficult for them to grasp and to teach. What Soccer Transition Training: Moving Between Attack and Defense *provides the reader with is insight, detail on the topic, and extremely useful and practical training activities and methodologies to explore with players and ultimately improve performance. Tony and John have provided tools for the coach to become more effective and to be able to recognize and train key moments in the game. These key moments occur at the highest level of the game and typically more frequently at the grassroots level, through club, to high school to college. There is something in this book for all coaches seeking to do better for their players, improve performance, and help the evolution of the global game."*

Ian Barker, Director of Coaching Education, United Soccer Coaches

"The only resource you need to start mastering one of the most critical components of the modern game. Informative, practical and packed with examples of training exercises to implement with any team, at any level."

Ashley Wallace, Performance Analyst, Sporting Kansas City (MLS)

"I am sincerely appreciative of the opportunity to offer an endorsement to this great piece of work by Tony and John, both of whom I met during the NSCAA Master of Coaching Course at the University of Delaware.

My mind goes back to 1994 when I traveled with a group of NSCAA coaches to the Netherlands to participate in the KNVB's Foreign Trainers Coaching Course. It was here that the importance of "the moments of truth" was hammered home. Translated to moments of transition, this aspect of the game was considered by our Dutch teachers as being critically important in both talent identification and in the training of players.

The ASTRA Soccer Academy is entrusted with developing youth players for the Canadian High Performance Stream. Our task is to produce intelligent individuals who are able to read the game and to act and react with high levels of confidence with the goal of reaching top collegiate or national team status. The authors of this book have produced an important tool, full of principles and exercises that our coaches can use immediately in our academy. It is common for us to see young players who typically 'switch off' at these critical times. This tool will help our players move past this problem."

Percy Hoff, Director of Coaching and Player Development,
ASTRA Soccer Academy, Canada

Games at the highest level are often determined in moments of transition, and this book highlights every transitional aspect of the game and how to prepare your team to maximize their performance when the game is on the line. I have worked with John Pascarella in a professional setting, and the book reflects his and Tony Englund's commitment to sharing their passion for helping coaches and players understand this most challenging of coaching topics.

Davey Arnaud, First Team Assistant Coach, Houston Dynamo (MLS)